WRITERS AND THEIR WORK

ISOBEL ARMSTRONG
General Editor

BRYAN LOUGHREY
Advisory Editor

D0976133

David Lodge

DAVID LODGE

David
Lodge

Bernard Bergonzi

Northcote House

in association with
The British Council

First published in 1995 by Northcote House Publishers Ltd, Plymbridge House,
Estover Road, Plymouth PL6 7PZ, United Kingdom.
Tel: (01752) 735251. Fax: (01752) 695699.

British Library Cataloguing-in-Publication Data
A catalogue record for this book is available from the British Library

ISBN 0 7463 0755 1

Typeset by PDQ Typesetting, Stoke-on-Trent
Printed and bound in the United Kingdom by BPC Wheatons Ltd, Exeter

Contents

Acknowledgements   vi

Biographical Outline   vii

Abbreviations and References   viii

1   Early Novels   1

2   Tales of the Academy   13

3   Catholic Questions   29

4   Literary Criticism   48

5   Lodge and the Art of Fiction   58

Select Bibliography   62

Index   66

Acknowledgements

The author and publishers acknowledge with thanks David Lodge's assistance and co-operation in the preparation of this study; acknowledgements are also due to the publishers of his work and of other copyright material.

Biographical Outline

1935	Born in South London.
1952–5	Undergraduate, University College London.
1955–7	Military Service in Royal Armoured Corps; writes *The Picturegoers*.
1957–9	Postgraduate student.
1959	Marries Mary Jacob; employed by British Council.
1960	Lecturer in English, Birmingham University; publishes first novel, *The Picturegoers*.
1963	Collaborates with Malcolm Bradbury on revue at Birmingham Rep.
1964–5	Harkness Fellowship; studies at Brown University and tours USA.
1966	Publishes first critical book, *Language of Fiction*.
1969	Visiting Professor, University of California, Berkeley.
1975	*Changing Places* wins Hawthornden Prize and *Yorkshire Post* Fiction Prize.
1976	Professor of Modern English Literature, Birmingham University.
1980	*How Far Can You Go?* Whitbread Book of the Year.
1984	*Small World* shortlisted for Booker Prize.
1987	Retires from Birmingham University with title of Honorary Professor.
1988	*Nice Work* is *Sunday Express* Book of the Year; shortlisted for Booker Prize.
1989	Adapts *Nice Work* for television.
1991	*The Writing Game* performed at Birmingham Rep.
1994	Adapts *Martin Chuzzlewit* for television.
1995	Publishes tenth novel, *Therapy*.

Abbreviations and References

AB	*After Bakhtin* (London: Routledge, 1990)
AF	*The Art of Fiction* (London: Secker, 1992)
ANWT	'Adapting *Nice Work* for Television', in P. Reynolds (ed.), *Novel Images* (London: Routledge, 1993)
BMFD	*The British Museum is Falling Down* (London: Secker, 1981)
CP	*Changing Places* (London: Secker, 1975)
GYB	*Ginger, You're Barmy* (Harmondsworth: Penguin, 1982)
HFCYG	*How Far Can You Go?* (London: Secker, 1980)
LF	*Language of Fiction* (London: Routledge, 1966)
MMW	*The Modes of Modern Writing* (London: Arnold, 1977)
NAC	*The Novelist at the Crossroads* (London: Routledge, 1971)
NW	*Nice Work* (London: Secker, 1988)
NT	'The Novelist Today: Still at the Crossroads?' in M. Bradbury and J. Cooke (eds.), *New Writing* (London: Minerva, 1992)
OS	*Out of the Shelter* (London: Secker, 1985)
PN	*Paradise News* (London: Secker, 1991)
SW	*Small World* (London: Secker, 1984)
TP	*The Picturegoers* (Harmondsworth: Penguin, 1993)
WO	*Write On* (London: Secker, 1986)
WS	*Working with Structuralism* (London: Routledge, 1981)
Bergonzi 1	B. Bergonzi, 'David Lodge Interviewed', *The Month* (February 1970)
Bergonzi 2	B. Bergonzi, 'A Religious Romance: David Lodge in Conversation', *The Critic* (Fall 1992)

Eco   U. Eco *Semiotics and the Philosophy of Language* (Basingstoke: Macmillan, 1984)

Haffenden   J. Haffenden, *Novelists in Interview* (London: Methuen, 1984)

Kostrzewa   R. Kostrzewa, 'The Novel and its Enemies: A Conversation with David Lodge', *Harkness Report* (December 1993)

Moseley   M. Moseley, *David Lodge: How Far Can You Go?* (San Bernardino: Borgo Press, 1991)

Scholes   R. Scholes, *Textual Power* (New Haven: Yale University Press, 1985)

Tallis   R. Tallis, *Not Saussure* (Basingstoke: Macmillan, 1988)

Walsh   C. Walsh, 'David Lodge Interviewed', *Strawberry Fare* (Autumn 1984)

Widdowson   P. Widdowson, 'The Anti-History Men: Malcolm Bradbury and David Lodge', *Critical Quarterly* (Winter 1984)

Early Ghosts

1

Early Novels

David Lodge's first four novels, *The Picturegoers, Ginger, You're Barmy, The British Museum is Falling Down* and *Out of the Shelter* were published between 1960 and 1970. They contain settings and topics drawn from his own experience which were to recur in different guises in his subsequent work. These include South London suburbia; the academic world, particularly university English departments; Catholicism; and the attractions of the American way of life. The first two novels and the fourth are works of sober realism, but the third, *The British Museum is Falling Down*, brings together realism and farce and formal invention in a way that looks forward to Lodge's later novels.

The Picturegoers (1960) was published when Lodge was twenty-five, but had been completed two years earlier, and is a strikingly precocious achievement for so young a writer. The setting is the suburban milieu in which he grew up, here called 'Brickley', as opposed to the real-life Brockley, and the formal and thematic focus of the novel is a large local cinema, the Palladium, where the characters go for their Saturday night outings. *The Picturegoers* is precisely located in social history: in the mid-1950s cinema-going was still popular, as it had been in the thirties and forties, though it was under threat from television. The Palladium has come down in the world; once it had been a well-known variety theatre, and now, seedy and dilapidated, it is only just holding on as a cinema.

For the central characters, Saturday evening at the cinema is followed by Sunday morning at Mass. (Lodge has remarked that Alan Sillitoe's title *Saturday Night and Sunday Morning* would have suited his novel very well.) The Mallory family are Catholics, some fervent, some merely dutiful. Mr Mallory is an Englishman and a convert, but his wife is an Irishwoman, and they have had eight children. The eldest son is a priest, and another, still at

1

school, is expected to follow the same path. Their eldest daughter, Clare, is back at home after unsuccessfully trying to be a nun. Other people are brought into the story, because they know the Mallorys or spend Saturday nights at the Palladium. Lodge's presentation of this range of characters is ambitious and assured, taking us in and out of their consciousness, each in an appropriate idiom. In an essay on his debt to Joyce (*WO* 57–69), he has acknowledged the influence on *The Picturegoers* of the 'Wandering Rocks' section of *Ulysses*, where a variety of representative Dubliners pass and repass each other on the streets of the city.

Mark Underwood, a London University undergraduate, takes a room in the Mallory household. He, as it happens, is a lapsed Catholic of raffish and cynical temperament, who is soon captivated by the essential goodness and decency of the Mallory family. He takes out the former aspiring nun, Clare, a virginal but well-built girl, and to please her goes to Mass with her. There he finds his faith dramatically returning, as expressed in a simile echoing another of Lodge's early literary mentors, Graham Greene: 'The priest stretched up, lifting the Host on high. Mark stared at it, and belief leapt in his mind like a child in the womb' (*TP* 111). Mark's original intentions towards Clare were not particularly honourable, but before long she falls in love with him. Mark, though, is now thinking of a higher end, in the force of his returning faith: not Christian marriage but the celibate priest- hood. Clare has to sacrifice him gracefully. The novel's Catholic aspects now look schematic and exaggerated, and in his introduction to the 1993 reissue of the book Lodge has commented on how remote much of its religious dimension now seems to him. There is, though, an element of comic relief in the discomfiture of Father Kipling, who mistakenly finds himself sitting through a gangster movie with sexy interludes instead of, as he had been expecting, *Song of Bernadette*. I shall defer further discussion of Lodge's treatment of Catholic topics to a later section of this study.

The Picturegoers combines sharp observation, clever guesswork and literary indebtedness. It shows the realistic novelist's capacity to catch the telling and placing details of the appearance of things, and an acute ear for speech and dialogue. The guesswork comes in when the young author has to write about matters he has had no direct experience of, such as the happy and sexually fulfilled

2

marriage of the middle-aged Mallorys (Lodge was still unmarried when he wrote the book). And there are many literary echoes, from Joyce and Greene and more contemporary novelists. The author is out of his depth in his characterization of the Teddy Boy, Harry, a psychopath and potential rapist who seems to be derived from Pinkie in Greene's *Brighton Rock* rather than from observation of life. Harry is unconvincingly redeemed by meeting a nice girl who encourages him to dance in the aisles of the Palladium at a showing of the film *Rock Around the Clock*, a historical detail from the year 1956. What remains notable about *The Picturegoers* is not its inevitable unevenness but its extraordinary assurance in handling a complex narrative. This would have indicated at the time that its author would go on to greater things, even if it offered few clues about the direction he would take.

Lodge's second novel, *Ginger, You're Barmy* (1962), is a simpler story, much narrower in range. From the Second World War until the late 1950s, all able-bodied young men had to put in two years of military service. The system was generally unpopular, regarded by many of those who underwent it as a waste of time which did not usefully add to the military strength of the nation. The British have never had a tradition of peacetime conscription, unlike Continental countries where military service is an integral part of citizenship. Students had to decide whether to get their service in before going to university, thereby interrupting their studies, or to defer it, and have it hanging over them. Jonathan Browne, the central figure of the novel, follows the latter course, as did its author. In the Afterword to the 1982 reissue, Lodge wrote, '*Ginger, You're Barmy* cleaves very closely to the contours of my own military service. Although the story of the three main characters is fictional, there is scarcely a minor character or illustrative incident or detail of setting that is not drawn from the life' (*GYB* 213).

Jonathan Browne is cautious, ambitious, self-regarding and an agnostic; he detests the army but tries to make himself as comfortable as possible within the system (as, Lodge admits, he did himself). He is contrasted with his friend Mike 'Ginger' Brady, an impulsive young man from an Irish Catholic background who is a natural rebel, and falls badly foul of the military machine. The polarity between Jonathan and Mike is an early instance of Lodge's liking for opposed pairs of types or places. Jonathan

3

behaves shabbily towards Mike, who ends up in prison, having lost his girl, Pauline, to his friend.

Lodge admits that *Ginger, You're Barmy* was an act of deliberate revenge against the army. The blend of scrupulous realism, resentment at class distinctions and general bloody-mindedness gives the novel something in common with the work of the new English writers who emerged in the 1950s and were labelled as the 'Angry Young Men'. Its author, though, regards Graham Greene as the dominant influence, realizing after the book was written how much the structure owed to *The Quiet American*, and how the tone was often reminiscent of Greene; 'there is a sentence in the first paragraph of *Ginger* which strikes me now as quintessentially Greenian in its relishing of the paradoxes of the moral life, its cadenced syntax and resonant abstractions: "I could never again write so unflattering an account of myself as the following, because it would open up so many awful possibilities of amendment."' (*GYB* 215). There is, too, the occasional elaborate simile in the manner of Greene: 'It must have been a time when Mike was still very much the link between us, when we anxiously talked and corresponded about him, like two watchers conferring at the bedside of someone gravely ill, our fingers straying imperceptibly towards each other in the darkness of the sick-room' (*GYB* 123). In general, though, the narrative is plain and unsurprising. It does, however, have some memorable touches, like the young soldier called Norman, a minor character but an impressive comic creation, who moves noisily but uselessly through his army career, finally injuring his hand in a typewriter while training to be a clerk.

The main narrative of *Ginger, You're Barmy* is framed by a brief Prologue and Epilogue, in which Jonathan discusses the story a few years later and brings us up to date about subsequent events, when he tries to make amends to Ginger. Lodge has said that he used this framing device to distance Jonathan's unamiable qualities of envy, selfishness and deceit (*GYB* 214). I do not think it works very well, but the failure may be one of technique rather than of nerve. Jonathan's story might have been artistically richer if he were deliberately presented as an 'unreliable narrator', whose assessments of himself and others are not to be trusted. The device is interesting, though, as an early sign of Lodge's inclination to step outside the narrative, to signal an awareness that it is a story and not a simple slice of life, anticipating the more sophisticated self-consciousness of his later novels.

The Picturegoers and *Ginger, You're Barmy* offer the pleasures of skilled story-telling and remain worth reading. They are also fascinating for describing a world that in some ways is remarkably different from our own; when, as Lodge has remarked, the concepts of racism and sexism did not exist; and when well-brought up young men, as well as young women, were expected to remain virgins until marriage, and often did so, whether from principle or lack of opportunity. The Dionysiac release provided by the rock'n'roll movie at the end of *The Picturegoers* was an unrecognized herald of changes to come. In 1962, after Lodge had published his second novel, it could have seemed that there was now nowhere for him to go. Writing in a vein of scrupulous and observant realism, he had used up a lot of experience: a Catholic childhood and family life in *The Picturegoers* and student days and military service in *Ginger, You're Barmy*. He became a lecturer in English at Birmingham University in 1960, and the routines and predictability of academic life might not have offered the stuff of interesting fiction. If Lodge had stopped then, he would not have been the first talented young writer to begin with a couple of promising novels and then give up, whether to become a critic or scholar, or to follow some non-literary career.

In the event, though, he showed himself to possess not only the staying power but the inventiveness to go on writing, and to write a different kind of fiction. Despite occasional humorous passages and a gently ironic tone, there is not much in the first two novels to suggest that Lodge could become a wholeheartedly comic novelist, as he did in *The British Museum is Falling Down* (1965). He has described how he did so. At Birmingham he collaborated with his then colleague Malcolm Bradbury and another friend in writing a satirical revue which was put on at the Birmingham Rep in 1963: 'I discovered in myself a zest for satirical, farcical and parodic writing that I had not known I possessed; and this liberated me, I found, from the restrictive decorums of the well-made realistic novel' (*BMFD* 6).

The British Museum is Falling Down is a very funny book about a potentially grave subject. In *The Picturegoers* Lodge had painted an idealized picture of Catholic family life, but here the realities are bleaker. Adam Appleby, a penurious Catholic graduate student, already has three small children and is afraid that a fourth may be on the way. As loyal Catholics he and his wife are restricted in their family planning to the elaborate and unpredictable system known as the 'rhythm method' or 'safe period', which involves complex operations with calendar and temperature chart. On the single day in which the novel is set, his wife's period is already ominously late. *The British Museum is Falling Down* appeared at a time when many Catholics entertained hopes – subsequently disappointed – that the ban on contraception would be lifted, and it reflects their state of mind. Those outside the Catholic Church meanwhile regarded the topic with amused or puzzled interest, and Lodge's novel ministered to their curiosity. He remarked that the problem 'seemed to me a part of experience which could only be treated comically if it were not to be tedious, and rather absurd' (Bergonzi 1, 112).

Adam spends his days in the great domed Reading Room of the British Museum (now known as the British Library, and due to move to a new building), where he is working on a thesis about style in the modern English novel. The treatment of sex in the literature he reads contrasts with his own anxious experiences, and he says of the difference between literature and life: 'Literature is mostly about having sex and not much about having children. Life is the other way round' (*BMFD* 65). (This aphorism has since found its way into dictionaries of modern quotations.) Like *Ulysses*, *The British Museum is Falling Down* is confined to the events of a single day, and is centred on the Reading Room, though in fact Adam spends very little time reading. He takes a pub lunch with friends, attends a meeting of a Catholic society, visits his academic supervisor, and is caught up in a wild-goose chase in pursuit of the papers of a long-dead Catholic writer, which might provide a scholarly coup and gain him an academic job. Events follow each other with farcical rapidity: there is a false fire alarm in the museum, for which Adam is unwittingly responsible; for a time he is lost in the library stacks; and a precocious schoolgirl, daughter of the custodian of the papers he is after, tries to seduce him in exchange for handing them over, a proposition which tempts him, more out of ambition than out of lust, but which he finally resists. Throughout the day he is worried by his wife's possible pregnancy, which leads him to make many futile phone calls to her. Late that night, when Adam is asleep, her belated period starts; their immediate anxiety is lifted but the larger problem remains.

For many readers it is enough that *The British Museum is Falling Down* is a dazzling comedy with lively characters and sharp, witty language. Some will also have an interest in its Catholic aspects. And others, especially those professionally concerned with literature, will respond to its exploration of intertextuality, the sense that literature inevitably draws on other literature. Adam reflects that so much experience has already been used up by the great writers of the past, and his aphorism about the difference between life and literature is prompted by the accusation from one of his friends that he no longer knows what the difference is. In his 1981 introduction Lodge refers to what the critic Harold Bloom calls the Anxiety of Influence: 'the sense every young writer must have of the daunting weight of the literary tradition he has inherited, the necessity and yet seeming impossibility of doing something in writing that has not been done before' (*BMFD* 5). Adam, the research student, feels this anxiety, but it really belongs to his creator, the novelist; Lodge deals with it by weaving the problem into the narrative itself. At intervals Adam finds himself responding to the successive events and traumas of the day in the manner of a twentieth-century novelist. When he arrives at the museum in the morning he encounters bureaucratic obstruction on having to get his out-of-date reader's ticket renewed. It is the sort of situation that we readily describe as 'Kafkaesque', but Lodge actually writes it in the manner of Kafka. The talent for parody which he had discovered when contributing material to a stage revue is now directed to the ends of literary self-reflectiveness; Joyce had shown what could be done with the expressive use of parody in the 'Oxen of the Sun' section of *Ulysses*.

The authors parodied include such modern masters as Kafka, Conrad, James, Lawrence, Woolf, Hemingway, and some lesser figures, like C. P. Snow and Baron Corvo; the latter provokes a superb excursion into fantasy, when Adam imagines he has become pope and issues an encyclical permitting the faithful freedom of choice in the matter of contraception. Another Catholic writer, Greene, is invoked when Adam is lost in the stacks; 'He had crossed a frontier – there was no doubt of that; and already he felt himself entering into the invisible community of outcasts and malefactors – all those who were hunted through dark ways shunned by the innocent and respectable ... Show me the happy scholar, he thought, and I will show you the bliss of ignorance' (*BMFD* 99). Lodge had closely studied Corvo and Greene in the course of writing a monumentally long MA dissertation on Catholic writers; he also invents a convincing autobiographical fragment by Egbert Merrymarsh, the minor figure from the Chesterbelloc era whose papers Adam is after. His pursuit of Merrymarsh prompts one of the finest parodies, when his genteel tea with the author's middle-aged niece is rendered in the style of Henry James:

> It was with a, for him, unwonted alacrity that our friend, hearing the tinkle of china in the hall, sprang gallantly to the door.
>
> 'I've been admiring your "things",' he said, as he assisted her with the tea-trolley.
>
> 'They're mostly my uncle's,' she said. 'But one does one's best.' She gestured vaguely to a cabinet where reliquaries statuettes and vials of Lourdes water were ranged on shelves, dim dusty devotional.
>
> She made tea in the old leisured way, pouring the water into the pot from a hissing brass urn.
>
> 'One lump or...?' she questioned. (*BMFD* 115).

In conclusion Lodge turns to Joyce, to Molly Bloom's long unpunctuated soliloquy at the end of *Ulysses*, to provide a climactic parody, and to enable Barbara, Adam's wife, to move into the picture and have her say, and indeed the final word. We share her inner monologue as Adam, unaware that her period has started, lies asleep beside her. Molly Bloom's final word had been 'yes'; Barbara's is a tentative 'perhaps', which Lodge regards as 'more appropriate to Barbara's character and the mingled notes of optimism and resignation on which I wanted to end the novel' (*BMFD* 7).

Out of the Shelter (1970), published five years later, is a very different kind of book. It does not continue the wit, ingenuity and high spirits of *The British Museum is Falling Down*, but makes a determined return to traditional realism. The first edition was beset by all kinds of problems, both before and after publication, wryly described by Lodge in his introduction to the revised edition of 1985, where he put back cuts demanded by the original publisher and tried to restore the text to something like his original intentions. The book remains something of an oddity, not widely read, and is unlike the common conception of a David

Lodge novel. Nevertheless, it contains some of his best writing. It is Lodge's most directly autobiographical novel, and for this extended recreation of personal experience it seems that he needed to return to the straightforwardly realistic mode with which he began. We are back in the milieu of *The Picturegoers*, Catholic family life in the South London suburbs, but the treatment is more detached.

Timothy Young, the central figure, is 5 years old when the novel opens in 1940. The presentation of his consciousness is openly indebted to Joyce's *A Portrait of the Artist as a Young Man*: 'Soon he found out that war was a Mickey Mouse gasmask that steamed up when you breathed and his father getting a tin hat and a whistle and Jill crying because her father was going away to join the Air Force and the wireless on all the time and black paper stuck over the front-door windows and sirens going and getting up in the middle of the night because of the raids. It was fun getting up in the middle of the night' (*OS* 3). Timothy enjoys the snug warmth of the air-raid shelter in the garden. A bomb falls nearby, killing his little playmate and her mother and half burying the shelter with rubble; but Timothy does not want to leave it: 'In the end, one of the men carried him, kicking and screaming, out of the shelter, into the open air.' The implications of this sentence echo throughout the novel.

Lodge is systematically indebted to *A Portrait* in this book, even following Joyce's Continental convention of beginning dialogue with a dash instead of enclosing it in quotation marks. In 'My Joyce', he acknowledges *Out of the Shelter*'s debt to *A Portrait*, and also to the rigorous naturalism of *Dubliners*, but admits that he falls far short of the model: '*Out of the Shelter*, however, plays much safer than *A Portrait* in both surface and deep structure. It quite lacks the bold variation of styles, the poetic rhythms and leitmotifs, the disconcerting temporal gaps, and the uncompromising allusiveness of Joyce's masterpiece' (*WO* 68).

Timothy, as he grows up, cannot claim the poetic sensibility of Stephen Dedalus, but he has some affinities with him; he is a timid but brainy lad who attends the local Catholic grammar school, where he is hardworking and somewhat priggish, but is kept in touch with the rest of humanity by his interest in sex and football. Lodge skilfully sketches in the various influences on the growing boy: a narrow maternal possessiveness, anxious suburban respectability, and a rigid, rather superstitious form of Catholicism. Meanwhile the war drags on, until 1945 finally brings peace and what Timothy sees as the sudden mysterious replacement of the great war leader Churchill by the colourless Attlee. Shortages and hardships seem unending, and the ministers in the Labour government, Strachey, Shinwell and Cripps, are demonized, replacing the grosser bogeymen, Hitler, Goebbels and Goering. Lodge filters public events through the consciousness of the boy, and effectively catches the climate of feeling of the immediate postwar period.

The greater part of the narrative occurs when Timothy is 16, in 1951. His much older sister, Kate, has already moved out of the shelter of the family, and works as a secretary for the American army in Germany. She has not been home for several years, though she regularly sends back American luxuries and consumer goods, and she invites Timothy to join her for a holiday; with timid eagerness on his part, and many misgivings on his parents', he accepts. What happens to him during his stay in Heidelberg provides a significant rite of passage. Germany itself is not much more than a background: impressions of Old Heidelberg, a sense of Wagnerian menace, crippled ex-soldiers, and wartime nightmares about Hitler (though the city itself escaped war damage, which is why the Americans made it their headquarters). The real impact on Timothy comes from the way of life of the American occupying forces: huge steaks, huge cars, and a bewildering and seductive variety of ice-cream sodas in a drug-store. In every sense, this is rich fare for the naïve and sheltered schoolboy who has just come from the physical shortages and imaginative poverty of postwar England. Even in his dealings with his sister, who is genuinely pleased to see him, culture shock is mixed up with adolescent uncertainties. Timothy upsets her by declining her offer of a shower after his long and tiring train journey, saying that he had had a bath two nights before; he is accustomed to a weekly bath whereas Kate now takes daily showers.

He learns a lot as he emerges from the shelter, and the reader shares the boy's sense of himself as absurd as well as vulnerable. An older woman offers to have sex with him, but he nervously declines; in the end he achieves a kind of sexual initiation when he is masturbated by a worldly but good-hearted American high school girl, as the climax of a bout of heavy petting (another

10

characteristic American custom, at least at that time). One of Lodge's critics, Merritt Moseley, has shrewdly remarked, 'It is a mark of Lodge's control, I believe, that he does not give Timothy the complete sexual success which is a feature, and a very unconvincing one, of so many adolescent-coming-of-age stories' (Moseley, 48).

In the character of Timothy, Lodge shows an acute and sensitive understanding of adolescence. He drew on some of his own youthful experiences; but at the same time Timothy has an archetypal quality, recalling Candide, and the aspiring young men in French and English novels of the nineteenth century who learn to pick their way over social and cultural obstacles as they rise in the world. Lodge has said, 'I tried to write a really ambitious socio-cultural novel, in the form of a *Bildungsroman*: it didn't quite come off, but that was the motivation' (Haffenden, 151). In fact, *Out of the Shelter* is only a *Bildungsroman* in a very truncated sense. That mode usually shows the hero moving from youth to early manhood – as in Joyce's *Portrait* or Lawrence's *Sons and Lovers* – but in this novel Lodge skips over that phase. We leave Timothy at the age of 16, and encounter him again in the Epilogue; when he is 30, a successful academic who is touring the United States on a fellowship, with his wife and two children. He is visiting Kate, who now lives in America, and he is gratifying to the full the taste for things American that he first acquired in Heidelberg.

In some respects, Kate is a more interesting character than Timothy, if only because she is older and has got out of the shelter sooner, notwithstanding the pain it causes her parents. Lodge uses her as the focus for a sharp critique of the material and mental smallness of the lower-middle-class suburban world in which she grew up, in the tradition of earlier writers like George Gissing, H. G. Wells and George Orwell. In Heidelberg Kate leads an artificially comfortable life, away from the privations of postwar England and cocooned from the devastation of postwar Germany. But she comes to realize that the expatriate American world is a dangerously unreal community, and that some of her friends are caught up in sexual and financial corruption. She escapes the unreality by emigrating to America itself. As Lodge has indicated, *Out of the Shelter* offers an updated version of the 'international theme' of Henry James's fiction, though here the representatively innocent figure is English rather than American

(*OS* ix). In a larger historical context, it dramatizes the impact, physical and imaginative, of American mass culture on English (indeed, European) life and values. Lodge's own early fascination with America comes across in the Epilogue to the novel, which I find a somewhat contrived bringing together of its scattered themes. This fascination is described in his autobiographical essay, 'The Bowling Alley and the Sun' (*WO* 3-16), and was to be brilliantly embodied in his next novel, *Changing Places*. The major achievement of *Out of the Shelter* is its sharp but moving presentation of a restricted childhood, and an adolescent consciousness trying to overcome the limitations of family and environment. Lodge has not attempted anything quite like this in his other novels; these may be experiences which could be written about only once.

2

Tales of the Academy

Traditionally, universities had featured in English fiction only in the kind of *Bildungsroman* which shows a young man's discovery of life – and himself – at an ancient university: examples include Thackeray's *Pendennis*, Compton Mackenzie's *Sinister Street*, and Evelyn Waugh's sharply contrasting *Decline and Fall* and *Brideshead Revisited*, with Rosamond Lehmann's *Dusty Answer* as a rare feminine instance. There was also the peculiarly Oxonian genre of the donnish detective novel. But there were other universities, in London and the provinces, though they did not appear in novels. The expansion of higher education after the Second World War meant that many more young people from lower-middle-class (and, less often, working-class) families went to university, though their attitudes and culture were remote from those traditionally associated with Oxbridge. The provincial and civic universities were now on the map, and in time provided the milieu for a new kind of fiction. As Lodge has described, he was one of the beneficiaries of the new educational opportunities:

> I was a classic product of the 1944 Education Act, the first generation who got free secondary schooling. A state-aided Catholic grammar school propelled me out of my class into the professional middle classes, and I went to read English at University College London. My school, I think, had never sent anyone to university before my year, and it couldn't give us much help: I didn't *know* there were universities other than Oxford, Cambridge and London. I didn't presume to apply to Oxford and Cambridge, so I applied to the local place. (Haffenden, 148)

Along with the growth of higher education went the expansion of English literature as an academic subject. Traditionally, would-be writers who went to university would take degrees in history or classics before embarking on a literary career. After the Second World War young men and women with literary interests and

13

aspirations would be more likely to read English. If they were clever enough they might stay on to do postgraduate work, and then become university teachers themselves, pursuing their writing on the margins of an academic career. David Lodge fitted into this pattern. He became a lecturer in English at Birmingham University in 1960, and was appointed Professor of Modern English Literature in 1976; he finally retired to write full time in 1987. During those years he successfully pursued a double career as a novelist and an academic literary critic.

The so-called 'campus-novel' emerged in America in the 1940s. America has many colleges and universities, and novelists have found a niche in them as teachers of creative writing. It is tempting to see, as many of them have done, the university as a microcosm of the large society, though often physically isolated from it, where academics, brought together in oppressive proximity, may be struggling with each other for power and promotion; or having affairs with their colleagues or colleagues' spouses, or their students. Power and sex, the traditional themes of fiction, are brought into high relief in the American campus novel. In England there were proportionally many fewer universities, and they did not offer the same opportunities for writers. But an English version of the campus novel made a lively impact when Kingsley Amis published his first novel, *Lucky Jim*, in 1954. It was a wonderfully comic work, but it had its serious implications, and it brought into public consciousness a new setting – a minor English provincial university – and a new kind of hero, the iconoclastic young man with good academic qualifications but a marked lack of sympathy for the traditional claims and attitudes of high culture. Lodge has acknowledged a substantial debt to Amis. There is a chapter on Amis in his first critical book, *Language of Fiction*, and in his Introduction to the Penguin edition of 1992 he re-examines *Lucky Jim* in a measured but still admiring way.

His own campus fiction is contained in three novels published between 1975 and 1988: *Changing Places, Small World* and *Nice Work*. They are set, partly or entirely, in the university and city of Rummidge, which he has said 'occupies for the purposes of fiction, the space where Birmingham is to be found on maps of the so-called real world' (*NW* v). Despite the continuity of places and of some characters, these three books were never planned as a trilogy; it was only when Lodge began work on *Small World* that he decided to make it a kind of sequel to *Changing Places*. Each novel remains formally and thematically distinct, though they were brought together in *A David Lodge Trilogy* in 1993.

Changing Places (1975) was a great success when it appeared, and it remains one of Lodge's best novels, triumphantly fulfilling the cosmic promise of *The British Museum is Falling Down*. It is funny, formally inventive, and technically sophisticated. Its subtitle is 'A Tale of Two Campuses' and on the first page the narrator describes it as 'this duplex chronicle'. The whole work is pervaded with doubleness and binary oppositions, features to which Lodge has always been inclined and which were given a new intellectual significance in the 1970s with the growing academic interest in structuralism (Jonathan Culler's influential *Structuralist Poetics* appeared in the same year as *Changing Places*). The tone is set by the opening sentences: 'High, high above the North Pole, on the first day of 1969, two professors of English Literature approached each other at a combined velocity of 1200 miles per hour. They were protected from the thin, cold air by the pressurized cabins of two Boeing 707s, and from the risk of collision by the prudent arrangement of the international air corridors. Although they had never met, the two men were known to each other by name' (*CP* 3). The two men, one British, one American, both aged 40, are Philip Swallow, a lecturer at Rummidge University, and Morris Zapp, a high-powered full professor at Euphoric State; this university, and the nearby city of Esseph and the surrounding state of Euphoria, bear much the same relation to Berkeley, San Francisco and the Bay area of California as Rummidge does to Birmingham. Swallow and Zapp are each about to start a half-year visiting appointment at each other's university, as part of an ongoing exchange arrangement between the two institutions.

The Englishman Swallow is a mild, amiable, unsophisticated teacher, 'unconfident, eager to please, infinitely suggestible'. He once wrote an MA dissertation on Jane Austen, but he loves the whole of English literature so much that he is unable to settle down to a specific 'research field'. He is eagerly looking forward to revisiting the United States, where he once spent a happy time on a travelling fellowship. The American Zapp is also a Jane Austen scholar, but he is a ruthless professional who has published several books on her, and wants to be the greatest expert on Jane Austen in the world, even though he personally dislikes her writing. He is one of the biggest guns on the Plotinus campus, and he has no great interest in Rummidge (or England, or indeed anywhere outside of America) but he has taken a visiting post there to escape from a marital crisis. Lodge uses the contrast between Zapp and Swallow – who will meet only in the final pages of the novel – to exploit to fine comic effect a whole series of oppositions: English and American academia; the Midlands and the Bay Area; clashing cultures in general.

While he is flying to England Zapp has the disturbed realization that he is the only male passenger – he has bought a cheap charter ticket from one of his female students – and that all the rest are pregnant women flying on a package tour to have abortions in England, where the law is more liberal than in Euphoria. Zapp's reaction reflects the serious as well as the farcical aspects of the situation:

> For Morris Zapp is a twentieth-century counterpart of Swift's Nominal Christian – the Nominal Atheist. Underneath that tough exterior of the free-thinking Jew (exactly the kind T. S. Eliot thought an organic community could well do without) there is a core of old-fashioned Judaeo-Christian fear-of-the-Lord. If the Apollo astronauts had reported finding a message carved in gigantic letters on the backside of the moon, *'Reports of My death are greatly exaggerated,'* it would not have surprised Morris Zapp unduly, merely confirmed his deepest misgivings. At this moment he feels painfully vulnerable to divine retribution. He can't believe that Improvidence, old Nobodaddy, is going to sit placidly in the sky while abortion shuttle-services buzz right under his nose, polluting the stratosphere and giving the Recording Angel writer's cramp, no sir, one of these days he is going to swat one of those planes right out of the sky, and why not this one? (*CP* 24)

The passage moves easily from the mode of the omniscient author to Zapp's own pungent stream of thought. It is full of literary references, alluding within a few lines to Swift, T. S. Eliot, Nietzsche, Mark Twain and Blake. Such allusiveness is typical of campus novels by teachers of English Literature; readers who pick up the references get additional pleasure, but those who do not need not be deflected from the story. Lodge has remarked, 'I write layered fiction, so that it will make sense and give satisfaction even on the surface level, while there are other levels of implication and reference that are there to be discovered by those who have the interest or motivation to do so' (Haffenden, 160).

Changing Places alternates rapidly between the respective adventures of Zapp in Rummidge and Swallow in Plotinus. Zapp is nearly overcome with cold and culture shock, but is tough enough to survive and find his way round in the arcane procedures, hilariously rendered, of English academic life; Swallow at Euphoric State finds that the West Coast at the end of the sixties is more surprising and rather more dangerous than the America he had idyllically experienced several years before. The novel's most obvious features are the wit and economy of language, and the rapidity and inventiveness with which the story proceeds. Lodge plays with modes of narrative in the carnivalesque spirit described by Bakhtin, a critic whom he later discovered and admired. Authorial description at the beginning of the novel gives place to the correspondence between Zapp and Swallow and their respective wives; in one of her letters, Swallow's wife, Hilary, says of a book on novel-writing that he has asked her to send him, 'There's a whole chapter on how to write an epistolary novel, but surely nobody's done that since the eighteenth century?' Then follows a section composed of newspaper reports and official university statements from Rummidge and Euphoric State as Zapp and Swallow get caught up in student unrest on either campus.

At the end of the novel, when Zapp and Swallow have not only exchanged jobs but had affairs with each other's wife, the four parties meet in New York to try to unravel the situation. This final episode is written as a film script, which opens with a variant of the opening image of the novel, as two Boeings come in to land at Kennedy airport, one bringing Swallow and Desirée Zapp from the West Coast, the other Zapp and Hilary from England: something goes wrong with the flight control and the planes almost collide ('I've always said, if God had meant us to fly he'd have given me guts,' says Zapp, mopping his brow). In the final pages, the two couples are sitting in a hotel room, talking about sex and history and literature, and trying to resolve their personal situations. Zapp quotes Jane Austen's words near the end of *Northanger Abbey*, to the effect that the reader is well aware that the novel is coming to an end: 'Seeing in the tell-tale compression of the pages before them that we are all hastening together to perfect felicity'. Swallow replies that that is true of a book but that in a film, especially a modern film, there are no such clear signals that the end is approaching. It can end anywhere, at any time; the last line of the novel is, 'PHILIP shrugs. The camera stops, freezing him in mid-gesture'.

Changing Places is deliberately self-conscious, a critical reflection on the art of fiction as well as an enjoyable example of it. We end up not knowing what will happen to Morris and Desirée, Philip and Hilary, but the author was enough of an old-fashioned realist to show us in *Small World*. *Changing Places* is dominated by a pattern of binary oppositions, often of an ingenious and unexpected kind; yet within this pattern, so indicative of the author's will and interests (particularly in Anglo-American culture clashes), the characters are lifelike and free, in the central tradition of realistic fiction. It is at the same time a work of great formal ingenuity and allusiveness, and a story (or a 'tale' as the Dickensian subtitle calls it) of recognizable people in recognizable places, dealing with familiar human dilemmas. It is close to actual history in its account of the disputes about the 'People's Garden' at Plotinus, which is drawn from events at Berkeley when Lodge was a visiting professor there in 1969.

In *Small World* (1984) we return to Rummidge and the principal characters of *Changing Places* ten years on. Swallow and Hilary are together again, but Zapp and Desirée are now divorced. Swallow has had some modest academic success; he has published a book on Hazlitt, and has become a professor, mainly by stepping into a dead man's shoes (such a promotion of someone whose 'academic productivity' was so low might still just have happened in the 1970s; but not in later years). He is also more raffish and less innocent than in the earlier book, with a weakness for pretty girl students. Morris Zapp has overcome his fear of flying and is continually travelling on the global conference circuit. He has given up his ambition to say everything about Jane Austen that can possibly be said and is now a poststructuralist for whom literary meaning is endlessly elusive, always escaping the critic's net. In the earlier novel Swallow and Zapp represented two different modes of academic culture; now they stand for opposed views of literary study – traditional humanism versus radical theory.

Small World continues the allusiveness of *Changing Places* and takes it much further, into intertextuality, a comprehensive if imprecise term referring to all the ways in which one literary work incorporates, rewrites, continues, parodies, or otherwise draws on another, whether as a conscious strategy or by unconscious derivation. Literature has always done this, despite Romantic claims that the literary work should be a unique entity, but the practice became conspicuous in the modernist era of Eliot and Joyce. The Prologue to *Small World* begins with the famous opening lines to Chaucer's General Prologue to the *Canterbury Tales*. The author goes on to observe that the present-day equivalent to Chaucer's pilgrims is academics going to conferences: 'The modern conference resembles the pilgrimage of medieval Christendom in that it allows the participants to indulge themselves in all the pleasures and diversions of travel while appearing to be austerely bent on self-improvement' (*SW* xi).

Small World is subtitled 'An Academic Romance', and this phrase is explained in the epigraph from Nathaniel Hawthorne: 'When a writer calls his work a Romance, it need hardly be observed that he wishes to claim a certain latitude, both as to its fashion and material, which he would not have felt himself entitled to assume had he professed to be writing a Novel.' The novel opens in familiar realistic fashion, though, at a dull and ill-attended conference of English lecturers at Rummidge. Lodge provides a painfully recognizable account of the corrosive boredom afflicting the audience as they sit through a lecture on Chaucerian metrics:

> Persse yawned and shifted his weight from one buttock to another in his seat at the back of the lecture-room. He could not see the faces of many of his colleagues, but as far as could be judged from their postures, most of them were as disengaged from the discourse as himself. Some were leaning back as far as their seats allowed, staring vacantly at the ceiling, others were slumped forwards onto the desks that separated each row, resting their chins on folded arms, others again were sprawled sideways over two or three seats, with their legs crossed and arms dangling limply to the floor. In the third row a man was surreptitiously doing *The Times* crossword, and at least three people appeared to be asleep. (*SW* 13)

Morris Zapp arrives, having just flown in from America, and enlivens some of the audience and scandalizes others with a scatological lecture called 'Textuality as Striptease' (which offers, in fact, a dazzling exposition of poststructuralist poetics). He does not stay long before dashing off to his next academic port of call in Italy, but he first meets and befriends the young Irish scholar and poet, Persse McGarrigle, who is red-haired, idealistic and remarkably innocent (reminiscent of the heroes of G. K. Chesterton's novels). Persse is the notional protagonist of *Small World* and he falls instantly in love with a mysterious young woman named Angelica who is attending the conference, though no one knows anything about her. She is as learned as she is beautiful, well acquainted with contemporary critical theory, and is working on a thesis on Romance. At this point the major intertextual elements of the novel become explicit.

Romance is one of the topics frequently talked about in *Small World*, and at the same time, as Lodge explains in his discussion with Haffenden, it inspired the spirit and form of the book. Angelica is partly derived from the princess of that name who is a leading character in Ariosto's sixteenth-century romance epic *Orlando Furioso*. 'Persse' is a variant of Percival, who is prominent in the Arthurian stories (with Wagner's Parzival as another version). Lodge has said, 'Percival in the myth is a knight who has very humble origins, and he's also very pure, a virgin' (Haffenden, 163). Persse's surname, McGarrigle, means 'Son-of-super-valour'. He will spend the rest of the novel pursuing Angelica but she is infinitely elusive. ' "Was there ever such a girl for disappearing?" he muttered to himself in vexation. "It's as if she had a magic ring for making herself invisible" ' (*SW* 45). As Lodge reminds us, Ariosto's Angelica had just such a ring, to which Persse may or may not be alluding; not all that many readers will get the particular reference, but invisibility is a common folklore motif (Walsh, 11).

After the opening in dismal Rummidge, the story takes off, in every sense, and becomes global. Many more characters appear, high-flying academics from different countries, hastening to or from conferences in all parts of the world. The magic horses which transport the constantly travelling characters in Ariosto are now jet aircraft. Jokes and comic episodes abound; even more than in *Changing Places* the spirit is carnivalesque. The story moves forward with the rapid movement and quick alternations of scene that characterize Lodge's comic fiction. He has said, 'As I worked at *Small World* I became more and more interested in the romance idea, weaving in as many romance motifs as I could, and I very deliberately exploited the narrative codes of mystery and suspense. I wanted to have a lot of enigmas and moments of uncertainty, and if you have a good many characters you can naturally create suspense by leaving one character and moving to another' (Haffenden, 162). *Small World* enacts ideas about the nature of narrative that Lodge was interested in as a critic; despite the prevailing air of fantasy and mystery it also contains a substantial amount of travelogue-fiction, with episodes in New York, Tokyo, Lausanne, Turkey, Hawaii, Israel, South Korea.

Orlando Furioso, with its rapid narrative and changes of scene over the known world, is one of Lodge's major models, as he acknowledges. He is misleading, though, when he says that the titillating scene of a knight rescuing a naked girl is repeated 'again and again', for there are only two such episodes (in Cantos 10 and 11, when first Angelica and then Olympia are offered, Andromeda-like, as victims to the sea monster Orc). (Haffenden, 163). It is revealed late in *Small World* that the high-minded and intellectual Angelica is one of a pair of identical twins who have been abandoned in infancy and brought up by a rich man. (Later still their parentage is dramatically revealed.) The other twin is a stripper who has performed in sex movies, and whose name is Lily Papps, in allusion to one of the two naked damsels disporting in the Bower of Bliss in Book II of Spenser's *Faerie Queene*:

> her two lily paps aloft displayed,
> And all, that might his melting heart entice
> To her delights, she unto him bewrayd:
> The rest hid underneath, him more desirous made.

Persse cannot tell the girls apart, and it is Lily, pretending to be Angelica, who steamily deprives him of his long-treasured virginity. Persse/Percival is only one of several Arthurian motifs in *Small World*. Zapp falls, almost fatally, into the clutches of Fulvia Morgana, an Italian Marxist professor of cultural studies, who is very rich and sexually insatiable; she is a latter-day version of Morgan le Fay of the Arthurian cycles, mentioned in Ariosto as Morgana. Arthur Kingfisher, the distinguished elderly doyen of literary critics, is impotent, and easily identified with the Fisher King, familiar to readers of Eliot's *Waste Land*. Zapp, Morgana, Kingfisher and several other senior academics are all in pursuit of *Small World's* version of the Holy Grail, the UNESCO Chair of Literary Criticism, a highly paid and prestigious appointment

21

with no particular duties, that will not even involve the successful candidate moving from his or her own university.

Despite Lodge's adroit exploitation of the multiple elements of romance and myth, *Small World* stays in touch with the realities of institutionalized literary study. Not that it is a faithful account of the daily lives of university teachers of literature, whether in Britain or elsewhere; even in 1979 very few had the opportunities for international conference-going that come the way of Lodge's characters. All that side of the novel is deliberately exaggerated. But it does dramatize the problems of a discipline pulled in many directions by the advent of literary theory. The characters embody contrasting attitudes to the subject, from young Persse, intellectually as well as morally innocent, to Swallow, a beleaguered defender of traditional empiricism and humanism, to the various modes of intellectual sophistication represented by Zapp and the Continentals. Lodge regards his characters genially, as figures of fun rather than objects of satirical mockery; the only one who attracts real animus is Rudyard Parkinson, a pompous, self-seeking and malicious Oxford don, an anglicized South African who reviews continually in metropolitan journals.

The novel ends in a mood of general reconciliation: marriages which have been coming apart are put together again, and other people announce their intention of getting married, including Zapp (for the third time), and Kingfisher, who gains the UNESCO Chair and whose virility is now restored. These unions recall the romance mode of Shakespearean comedy, but for Persse there is no such happy closure. He has lost Angelica, who is engaged to a Harvard academic; but on the last page he is off again in pursuit of another elusive female. This reflects a different mode of romance; Lodge remarks of Persse's continuing quest: 'I also remembered Northrop Frye's observation that in its most primitive form romance doesn't end: a character has one adventure after another until the author dies of exhaustion. So I left Persse still questing; it's not negative because it leaves the reader with a sense that he is off on another adventure' (Haffenden, 162). *Small World*'s global themes have gained it an appreciative international readership: Umberto Eco, in his preface to the French translation, defines it as an 'academic picaresque', and calls it one of the funniest novels of the century.

The action of *Nice Work* (1988) is confined to Rummidge. It is less continuously funny than *Changing Places* and *Small World*, and it lacks the obviously metafictional or carnivalesque devices of those books. In some respects it is Lodge's most conventionally realistic novel since *Out of the Shelter*. But the realism is self-consciously sustained. There is a wealth of intertextual references – mainly to Victorian fiction – and the book has the oppositional structure of some of his earlier novels. After the fantasy and myths of *Small World*, *Nice Work* is firmly rooted in contemporary history. The previous novel was set in 1979, the year in which the Conservative government of Margaret Thatcher came to power in Britain; *Nice Work* takes us seven years on, and shows the effects of the Thatcherite culture of market forces and competition, cuts in public expenditure, and general anti-intellectualism; primarily on the city and university of Rummidge, but by implication on society at large.

We meet some familiar figures. Philip Swallow has become an ageing senior academic, cynical, harassed, and intermittently deaf, who is desperately trying to cope with the managerial and philistine attitudes which now dominate the university. Morris Zapp flies in to make a welcome vignette appearance. But the two main characters are new creations, convincing both as individuals and as representative types. Vic Wilcox is an engineer turned businessman who has risen from humble beginnings by his own talents and hard work, and is now, in his mid-40s, managing director of a Rummidge engineering works. He is tough, impatient, energetic and very good at his job. He enjoys the material rewards of success, which include a Jaguar and a luxurious modern house with four toilets, a feature which scandalizes his elderly father. He loves his work, but away from it he is not particularly happy. Vic is intelligent but conscious of his cultural limitations; and he is emotionally and socially insecure. He has lost sexual interest in his wife, a woman of limited horizons who had once been a typist. She does not have a career, and is preoccupied with new consumer goods. When the Wilcoxes move into their new house she is enraptured with the *en suite* bathroom, as Vic sardonically recalls: '*I've always wanted an en suite bathroom*, she would say to visitors, to her friends on the phone, to, he wouldn't be surprised, tradesmen on the doorstep or strangers she accosted in the street' (*NW* 4). They have three teenage children who live at home and are lazy and unappreciative. Within Vic's consciousness, to which Lodge gives us full and frequent access, he is both a puritan and a romantic, who, as he drives to work, likes to play tapes of female singers with caressing, sexy voices. This is a very private pleasure, unknown to his family. Each day he passes Rummidge university, which is alien territory to him, his own early training having been severely practical and vocational. Early one morning, when the academics are holding a one-day strike, he notices two smartly dressed women on the picket line and scornfully thinks, 'So it's finally happened – designer industrial action'.

As fate, or rather the carefully designing author, would have it, Vic's life is about to become closely involved with one of these women. She is Dr Robyn Penrose, a temporary lecturer in English and Women's Studies. She is in her early 30s, attractive, sophisticated, a Sussex graduate with a Cambridge doctorate but with little hope of a permanent job in the financially stricken academic scene of the mid-eighties. She is both a dedicated teacher and a dedicated follower of the intellectual fashions of the time: Marxism, feminism, psychoanalysis, poststructuralism. When we first meet her she is reading items of progressive news in the *Guardian* 'with the kind of pure, trance-like attention that she used to give, as a child, to the stories of Enid Blyton'. Lodge presents her as likeable but naïve and narcissistic, and like many intellectuals remarkably ignorant of the way in which society actually works. She is an expert on the 'industrial novel' of the early Victorian period, but she knows nothing about industry. All this changes when, after pressure from Professor Swallow (himself under pressure from the Vice Chancellor), she reluctantly agrees to participate in a well-meaning but half-baked scheme intended to break down the barriers between the academy and the larger world outside. She is to spend one day a week in the company of the managing director of a local engineering works, as his 'shadow', accompanying him, watching and learning something about the ways of industry and commerce. The man in question is Vic Wilcox.

Nice Work tells the story of their enforced relationship as it extends over several weeks. It begins with resentment, hostility and ignorance on both sides, develops into mutual respect and understanding, and then into liking. During a business visit to Germany they have a brief, intense sexual encounter, initiated by

Robyn; Vic, unsophisticated in such matters, finds this a totally transforming experience, and insists that he is in love with her and wants to divorce his wife and marry her. But for Robyn it was a pleasurable one-night stand and no more. She is certainly not in love with Vic, though she remains fond of him, and in any case does not believe in romantic love. Lodge describes the developing relationship between Robyn and Vic with insight and humour. They learn a good deal about each other's world, as they were intended to, and it is Robyn who has to do the greater share of learning; Vic, after all, can remember a few works of literature which he read at school, while Robyn has never been in a factory, and takes her ideas of industry from the Victorian novels she studies and teaches. And her understanding of commerce and business is restricted to a few Marxist clichés.

For all its considerable human interest *Nice Work* is also a novel of ideas. The arguments between Vic and Robyn reflect their personalities, but they do more than that; they tap into a sustained debate in English culture about the effects of industrialism. Robyn is the heir to a distinguished intellectual tradition of hostility to industrial civilization, which extends from Carlyle to Leavis. Vic presents the opposing position that without national wealth, won in a harsh competitive world, none of the academic values and quality of life which Robyn takes for granted could be sustained. At the same time, he is becoming increasingly conscious of his own educational limitations and narrow horizons. Similar debates were enacted in the Victorian industrial novels, which were sometimes known, in Carlyle's expressive phrase, as 'Condition of England' novels; *Nice Work* is a latter-day addition to the genre. References to those books abound in Lodge's novel, in accounts of Robyn's teaching and scholarship, and in quotations from them which provide epigraphs to the separate sections. Several of the novels contain binary divisions akin to those in *Nice Work*: there is the opposition in Disraeli's *Sybil* between the 'two nations' of the rich and the poor; and in Dickens's *Hard Times* between the school and the circus, or more generally between head and heart; and, most fundamentally, the division indicated in the title of Elizabeth Gaskell's *North and South*. Lodge brings the argument up to date in the contrast between factory and university, industrialist and intellectual, practice and theory. Robyn and Vic embody these oppositions, whilst retaining their human uniqueness (a concept which Robyn, in theory, would probably want to reject on Marxist and poststructuralist grounds).

Writing as a critic Lodge has expressed the doubts about fictional realism that were in the air in the seventies and eighties, and the metafictional devices in his novels probe and question it. *Nice Work* suggest a carefully considered return to the conventions of Victorian realism. Lodge, like a conscientious nineteenth-century novelist, did a good deal of fieldwork in Birmingham factories and other industrial sites, and his imagination responded enthusiastically to the new subjects; to some degree his discoveries run parallel to Robyn's. There is an evident relish in the exact, fascinated presentation of domestic or public interiors, of clothes and furniture and other artefacts, and in catching revealing modes of speech, which has always been central in the appeal of the realistic tradition. This is not mere inert notation, as is alleged in conventional attacks on realism, but arises from a love of the endless variety of things and their surfaces. Lodge uses such descriptions as a means of establishing his characters' personalities and their ways of relating to their environments.

Some aspects of *Nice Work*, though amusing and precisely observed, are rather closely tied to their historical context and risk coming to seem dated. There is, for instance, the amiable satire on the Thatcher years in the account of Robyn's brother, Basil, who is doing very well for himself as a merchant banker, and his girl-friend Debbie, 'a pretty pale-faced girl with blonde hair cut like Princess Diana's and a figure of almost anorexic slimness', who is doing even better as a foreign exchange dealer. She is very expensively dressed, left school at sixteen, speaks with a Cockney accent and comes from a family of bookies in Whitechapel. On another level there is witty mockery of the fashionable interests of Robyn and her boy-friend Charles, another academic, in contemporary critical theory. Charles provides an unexpected twist to the plot when he gives up academic life to become a merchant banker, and in the process leaves Robyn for Debbie; he explains, 'I regard myself as simply exchanging one semiotic system for another, the literary for the numerical, a game with high philosophical stakes for a game with high monetary stakes...' (*NW* 225).

At the end of his novel Lodge pulls away from 'realism' as it is generally understood, which often (though not inevitably) implies a negative or gloomy conclusion of the kind common in late-nineteenth-century writers such as Gissing or Zola. *Nice Work* moves to a happy ending, rather in the spirit of the early Victorian novels which are invoked in it. Indeed, as with some of those works, it ends with more than a touch of romance or fairy-tale. Swallow finds that he may, after all, be able to give Robyn a permanent job; Morris Zapp reads the book she has been working on and recommends it for publication by his university press, boosting her career prospects; he even offers her a job at Euphoric State, but she prefers to stay at Rummidge. She also receives a handsome legacy from a dead uncle in Australia. Vic has been made redundant following a take-over of his company, and Robyn uses her new fortune to set him up in a business of his own; his wife will work as his secretary and he has hopes of restoring his failing marriage. Such emphatic closure is new in Lodge's fiction. The happy ending may indeed be something of an affront to the expectations of the readers of realistic fiction, but the author introduces his Victorian plot devices defiantly, in an ironic rebuff to Robyn, who has said in a lecture, 'all the Victorian novelist could offer as solution to the problems of industrial capitalism were: a legacy, a marriage, emigration or death' (*NW* 52). In the event, Robyn gets a legacy and uses it to set up a small-scale industrial capitalist. The conclusion of *Nice Work* may depend more on convention and genre than on probability, but the work is a comedy, and we expect comedies to end more or less happily.

Lodge presents the arguments between Vic and Robyn very even-handedly. It may be significant that *Nice Work* was published in 1988, the year after he gave up the university after twenty-seven years as a teacher. His earlier campus novels had been confined to the academy, but in this one, like Robyn, he steps outside it and finds a world elsewhere, as he did in real life. The professional writer, unlike the academic, is a solitary producer and directly dependent on the market; and thus more likely to understand the problems of other kinds of producer. One can make another cross-reference to Robyn's lecture, in which she remarks, 'the novelists were in a sense capitalists themselves, profiting from a highly commercialised form of literary production'. Robyn wants to stay in the academy, but Charles leaves it for what he regards as the more lucrative game-playing of the markets. He is a minor, reclusive and not altogether attractive character, but the long letter

27

he sends to Robyn announcing his change of careers – a profitable change, since he has taken a large sum in severance pay – contains some serious thoughts on the state of British universities in the 1980s, which Lodge himself later developed in an article ('Pay as You Learn', *Listener*, 5 October 1989). Charles expresses the sense of crisis that is pervasive amongst academics in literary study, but not often so openly admitted:

> Poststructuralist theory is a very intriguing philosophical game for very clever players. But the irony of teaching it to young people who have read almost nothing except their GCE set texts and *Adrian Mole*, who know almost nothing about the Bible or classical mythology, who cannot recognise an ill-formed sentence, or recite poetry with any sense of rhythm – the irony of teaching them about the arbitrariness of the signifier in week three of their first year becomes in the end too painful to bear... (*NW* 225)

Charles's letter leaves Robyn both angry and confused, echoing Stephen Blackpool in *Hard Times*: 'there were things in this letter which struck a nerve of reluctant assent, mixed up with things she found false and obnoxious. 'Twas all a muddle' (*NW* 226). Comedy and story-telling apart, Lodge's campus novels raise some searching questions about the academic study of literature.

3

Catholic Questions

There is a distinguished roll-call of English writers who have been Roman Catholics: Newman, Hopkins, Chesterton, Waugh, Greene, David Jones, Muriel Spark. But nearly all of them were converts to Catholicism. This fact separates them from the majority of their co-religionists, the 'cradle-Catholics' whose religion was passed on from their families, and, who, apart from a small number of upper-class 'Old Catholics', were working class or lower middle class, with a strong admixture of Irish immigrants. Their educational attainments and ambitions tended to be limited, and did not often turn them towards literature. Young people from such a background who took advantage of new educational opportunities and became socially mobile often abandoned Catholicism in the process. This has long been the case with Irish writers, most famously Joyce, though his work remained profoundly marked by the religion which he had abandoned. A number of recent English writers have been lapsed Catholics, who look back on Catholicism with affection or hostility, or elements of both. Examples include John Braine and Anthony Burgess, both of Northern English Catholic origin, and a succession of women authors seeking revenge for their convent education.

David Lodge is unusual in being a cradle-Catholic from a lower-middle-class family in South London who is a successful writer and who continues to regard himself as a Catholic, though his ideas about religion have changed greatly over the years. In 'Memories of a Catholic Childhood' (WO 28–32) he described his origins, which were not altogether typical of cradle-Catholic culture, since he was an only child and his father was not a Catholic:

My mother was a dutiful but undemonstrative daughter of the Church. I was given a Catholic schooling, but the atmosphere of the home was not distinctively Catholic. There was no great profusion of holy pictures and statues in the house, religion was a topic rarely touched on in conversation, and there was little of the regular and complex social interaction with parish clergy and laity that is a feature of the typical large devout Catholic family. I had no brothers or sisters to reinforce the Catholic cultural code, and my friends in the same street happened not to be Catholic. The result was that as a child I always felt something of an outsider in the Church, anxious to belong, to be accepted, yet hanging back on the periphery through shyness, absence of familial pressure and inadequate grasp of the relevant codes.

The sense of being in the Church and at the same time something of an outsider can be traced in Lodge's novels, which combine detailed knowledge of the institution with cool observation. At school he acquired an idea of the theological foundations of Catholic belief and developed 'a respect for and fascination with its subtleties and complexities'. Reading Joyce and other modern authors extended his intellectual horizons: 'I became more critical of the Catholic "ghetto" culture that I encountered in the parish and at school, especially its suspicious hostility towards the arts. When I discovered *A Portrait of the Artist as a Young Man* I identified immediately with Stephen Daedalus, though I had neither the courage nor the urge to rebel on so spectacular a scale'. Graham Greene and François Mauriac and other authors offered new possibilities within a Catholic world-view, 'presenting authentic religious belief as something equally opposed to the materialism of the secular world and to the superficial pieties of parochial Catholicism'. They drew the sinner as a representative Christian in a way that was exciting to an adolescent with literary ambitions: 'being a Catholic need not entail a life of dull, petty-bourgeois respectability. The extreme situations and exotic settings on which these writers thrived were, however, very remote from my experience; and when I came to try and write fiction for myself I domesticated their themes to the humdrum suburban-parochial milieu that I knew best'.

Lodge's first four novels all contain Catholic characters, but he does not put them through high spiritual dramas. His interest is much more in the subculture of English (or Hiberno-English) Catholics and their dealings with the rest of society. The problems that arise from following their beliefs are more likely to be treated comically than melodramatically. In *The Picturegoers* he presented 'the typical large devout Catholic family', with an Irish mother and an English convert father, basing it on his wife's family rather than his own. Kingsley Amis in a favourable review of *The Picturegoers* described it as 'a Catholic novel, but written without the nose-to-the-grindstone glumness, all sin and significance, that the phrase often implies'. Amis rightly praised Lodge's 'social eye': here and in his other early novels the frame of reference is sociological rather than theological, with much close observation of the minutiae of lower-middle-class Catholic life. When Mark Underwood first enters the Mallory household, he soon encounters the signs of Catholic devotion: 'the plastic holy water stoup askew on the wall, the withered holy Palm, stuck behind a picture of the Sacred Heart which resembled an illustration in a medical text-book, and the statue of St Patrick enthroned upon the dresser' (*TP* 44). This milieu has rarely been caught in English fiction, for the convert Catholic writers had little knowledge of it, and the closest parallels are in Joyce's domestic interiors.

Though the implied attitudes in *The Picturegoers* are entirely orthodox, in ways that seemed remote to Lodge when he wrote his preface to the 1993 reissue, there are elements of distancing irony directed at some of the more extreme manifestations of Catholic fervour. There is the odious Damien O'Brien, an Irish ex-seminarian who lives next door to the Mallorys and lusts after Clare. He is permeated with pharisaical piety, and Lodge gives him the malign vitality of a Dickensian caricature; he is described, in a Greene-ish simile as 'carrying his failure before him like a monstrance'. And there is Father Kipling, the parish priest of Brickley, who starts a campaign against the sinfulness of the cinema. He is an amiably ridiculous figure, whose portrayal suggests the mild anti-clericalism sometimes found in cradle-Catholics (more precisely, cradle-Catholic men).

In *Ginger, You're Barmy* the principal Catholic character is the Irish rebel, Mike Brady, to whom we never become very close, as we know him only through the narrative of his agnostic and ultimately disloyal friend, Jonathan Browne, who is dismissive of Mike's religion. He does, though, recall a poem Mike has written attacking contraception; an ironical touch, in the light of Lodge's next novel, *The British Museum is Falling Down*. That book broke entirely new ground for a Catholic novel, and despite its comic elements dealt with a serious subject: the ban on contraception and the restiveness that was beginning to be felt about it by married Catholics in the 1960s. Adam Appleby embodies the hopes that were in the air as the Second Vatican Council opened in 1962. Early in the story he gives a lift on his motor-scooter to Father Finbar, an *echt* Irish curate from his parish church, and tries to raise the possibility of a change in the teaching on birth control. Father Finbar will consider no such possibility; as far as he is concerned, the Church's teaching never changes on any subject whatsoever, and the true purpose of marriage is to procreate children and bring them up in the fear and love of God. Adam is hardly surprised, for he and his wife already regard him as the Priest Most Likely to Prevent the Conversion of England. Later in the day, he meets a priest of a very different kind, the radical Dominican, Father Bill Wildfire, who wears workmen's clothes and occupies dangerously advanced theological territory: 'I was preaching at a men's retreat the other day, and I told them, better sleep with a prostitute with some kind of love than with your wife out of habit. Seems some of them took me at my word, and the bishop is rather cross'. Father Wildfire is sympathetic to Adam's difficulties, but the priest's real concern is in larger spiritual dramas: 'In contrast, Adam's moral problem seemed trivial and suburban, and to seek Father Wildfire's advice would be like engaging the services of a big-game hunter to catch a mouse' (*BMFD* 72).

Father Finbar and Father Wildfire, contrasting caricatures as they are, reflect the divisions that were appearing in English Catholicism and which would deepen over the years. Finding no satisfaction, Adam retreats into his Corvine fantasy of becoming pope and decreeing all methods of birth control acceptable, with the result that 'so many lapsed Catholics are returning to the practice of their Faith that the Churches cannot accommodate them'. But in practice only the rhythm method, or safe period, was permitted to practising Catholics. Adam has already engaged in a fantasy about that, an imaginary article on 'Roman Catholicism' for a Martian encyclopaedia compiled after life on earth had been extinguished by nuclear war:

> Intercourse between married partners was restricted to certain limited periods determined by the calendar and the body-temperature of the

female. Martian archaeologists have learned to identify the domiciles of Roman Catholics by the presence of large numbers of complicated graphs, calendars, small booklets full of figures, and quantities of broken thermometers, evidence of the great importance attached to this code. Some scholars have argued that it was merely a method of limiting the number of offspring; but as it has been conclusively proved that the Roman Catholics produced more children on average than any other section of the community, this seems untenable. Other doctrines of the Roman Catholics included a belief in a Divine Redeemer and in life after death. (*BMFD* 16)

At the end of the novel, Adam's wife proves not to be pregnant after all, which brings immediate short-term relief, but the large issues remain unresolved. Lodge himself wrote in his Introduction to the new edition of 1981: 'Like most traditional comedy, *The British Museum is Falling Down* is essentially conservative in its final import, the conflicts and misunderstandings it deals with being resolved without fundamentally disturbing the system which provoked them. (That more fundamental disturbance is the subject of *How Far Can You Go?*)' (*BMFD* 3).

The British Museum is Falling Down was published in 1965, the year in which the Second Vatican Council completed its sessions. That great assembly of bishops from all over the world, called by Pope John XXIII to, in effect, update the Catholic Church, brought about many changes. Latin was replaced by the vernacular in much of the liturgy, theologians and scriptural scholars found a new freedom, and morality was seen less as adherence to rules laid down by an authoritarian system and more a matter of informed and responsible decision-making. The traditional modes of belief and practice described in *The Picturegoers* remained in place, but suffered noticeable and sometimes disturbing modification. Many conservative believers, of whom Evelyn Waugh was one of the most prominent, were distressed or angered by the changes. The Vatican Council did not, however, pronounce on contraception. That subject was removed from its deliberations by the pope and entrusted to a special commission made up of theologians, scientists and other experts. In time it voted by a large majority for a change in the traditional teaching, and such a change was widely expected. Nevertheless, in 1968 John's successor as pope, Paul VI, confuted expectations and reaffirmed the ban in his encyclical, *Humanae Vitae*. Instead of the resigned obedience which such a pronouncement might have prompted before the liberal climate initiated by Vatican II, there was a storm of protest. Married Catholics, at least in the western world, decided that if there was not to be a change in the law about contraception then they would ignore it. *Humanae Vitae* provoked a crisis not only about sexuality but about authority in the Church that is still unresolved.

How Far Can You Go? (1980) is a much more serious novel than *The British Museum is Falling Down*, in the senses of being both more intellectually and artistically ambitious and less funny, though it has its comic moments; Moseley says of it, 'This is the first novel... in which he has actually made being a Catholic a serious, world-historical kind of situation' (Moseley, 77). Lodge describes the enormous changes in the Church brought first by Vatican II and then by *Humanae Vitae* and the reaction to it, as they affect a group of middle-class English Catholics from the early 1950s, when they are students, to the late seventies, when some of them are no longer Catholics. Lodge said of the book in 1984:

> It was a subject nobody else seemed to have dealt with, what had happened to the Catholic Church over the last twenty-five years. Even the people in the Church haven't realized how it's changed out of all recognition, because it was a gradual change, and I needed a large number of characters in order to illustrate all the varieties of change – priests dropping out, for example, and nuns having to throw off their habits and adjust to the modern world; sexual problems in marriage, mixed marriages, changes in the liturgy – I would immediately think of a whole set of incidents and situations that I wanted to incorporate. It would have been a huge saga novel if I had treated it in a realistic mode. I also knew I had to find some way of communicating to a non-Catholic audience a lot of theological and ecclesiastical information. So thinking in terms of a short novel with a rather rapid pace, with a lot of characters and a lot of information to communicate, I was led inexorably to use a dominant, intrusive authorial voice which would communicate that information in a way I hoped was itself amusing. It meant cutting down the characterization to a fairly summary form, and having many characters of more or less equal importance. (Haffenden, 154–5)

In *How Far Can You Go?* Lodge departs from the realistic mode only in the limited sense that the novel rejects the Jamesian prescription that the author should always dramatize the story and go in for 'showing' rather than 'telling'. But the knowing story-teller, the dominant, intrusive, omniscient narrator, has been central in a line that runs from Cervantes to Fielding to the major Victorians; Thackeray, for instance, writes at the end of *Vanity Fair*, 'let us shut up the box and the puppets, for our play is played out'. This is every bit as deliberately alienated and distancing as the tone adopted by Lodge's narrator.

The opening of the novel is precisely located in history and geography. The year is 1952, it is 8 o'clock in the morning of a dismal February day – St Valentine's Day – in a sooty Catholic church in central London, where a group of London University students are attending Mass. These are the young Catholics whose fortunes we are to follow through the novel. There is Angela, pretty, blonde, and very devout, reading French. Dennis is a burly youth, reading chemistry, and not very devout; indeed, he is only at the Mass because he is in love with Angela. (They will marry, after a protracted, notionally chaste engagement lasting several years.) Polly is a dark, pretty girl, something of a rebel and destined to lose her virginity and her faith before long. She is reading English, and so is Michael, who is clever, sex-obsessed, and still a virgin, as are all of them at this point. He has a white face and dark greasy hair, and wears what the author piquantly describes as a 'wanker's overcoat'. After graduating Michael writes a thesis on Graham Greene, and references to Greene's new novels as they come out provide a subtext relating Lodge's work to an admired master of the English Catholic novel. Michael will marry Miriam, a convert to Catholicism, and have a happy marriage, though preserving a lively erotic imagination. Although Lodge has said that the characters are intended to be of roughly equal importance, in fact it is the married couples who are at the moral and imaginative centre of the novel: Angela and Dennis; Michael and Miriam; and, to a lesser extent, Edward, a somewhat lugubrious medical student who is acting as Mass server when we first see him, and Tessa, a nurse whom he marries after he qualifies as a doctor, and who willingly becomes a Catholic.

The other characters are more marginal. There is Adrian, a student of economics, who never really comes alive; theologically, he is a dogmatic conservative at the beginning of the book and a dogmatic liberal at the end of it. Ruth is a plain girl with a strong personality, reading botany; she is to become a nun and have an unexpectedly interesting life in the wake of the changes brought by Vatican II. Miles, a recent convert, is the only member of the group to have been at a public school; he becomes an academic historian and struggles with his homosexuality. Violet, reading classics, is a pretty but neurotic girl, who is to be seduced by a young lecturer and then marry him; her spiritual path takes her away from Catholicism, first to Jehovah's Witnesses, and then to Sufism. The person who travels the furthest is the young priest saying Mass. Initially, Father Austin Brierley is narrow-minded and priggish, but he will change enormously during the sixties and seventies. He is one of the priestly rebels against *Humanae Vitae*, but is handled gently by his bishop, who treats him as a managerial rather than a spiritual problem. Father Brierley is removed from parish work and sent on courses of study to keep him out of the way. He becomes more and more radical, discovering new modes of theology and biblical exegesis and moving into the secular discipline of sociology. By the end of the novel he has left the priesthood and married, though still considering himself 'a kind of Catholic'.

Throughout the novel Lodge keeps the focus on the group as a whole, cutting rapidly from one individual or couple to another, and freely using authorial omniscience to look ahead as well as back. Since there are a lot of characters, and *How Far Can You Go?* is not a long novel, their psychological and moral development over the years cannot be shown in any depth and one has to rely on the narrator to inform us about it (a matter of 'telling' rather than 'showing'). Indeed, they are not always sharply differentiated, a point which Lodge has accepted: 'One of the possible weaknesses of the book, which is an almost inevitable result of dealing with a homogeneous social group, is that the characters are likely to be confused with each other in the reader's mind' (Haffenden, 154). He has also acknowledged that the women characters tend to be more complex and interesting than the men; this is 'partly a reflection of the fact that in the period dealt with women have changed a lot more than men' (letter to the present writer, 6 June 1979).

One of the most important characters is the narrator, whose voice is frequently heard. In time it becomes evident that he is a version of David Lodge himself; he cross-refers to his other novels, and at the end of the book, when there is a round-up of what all the characters are doing, he says: 'I teach English literature at a redbrick university and write novels in my spare time, slowly, and hustled by history' (*HFCYG* 243). Such a device seems to undermine the distinction between 'fiction' and 'reality', but in fact the author-as-character is still an invented figure, and not identical with the historical individual whose name appears on the title-page. Wayne C. Booth provides a classic account of this question in *The Rhetoric of Fiction*; more recently, Lodge himself has written, 'the more nakedly the author appears to reveal himself in such texts, the more inescapable it becomes, paradoxically, that the author as a *voice* is only a function of his own fiction, a rhetorical construct, not a privileged authority but an object of interpretation' (*AB* 43). Although *How Far Can You Go?* is to a degree a formally innovative novel, its intervening, commenting narrator, who is ready to break off the story to insert little essays on religion or the nature of narrative, is reminiscent of Fielding's narrator in *Tom Jones*; he, too, has a pseudo-identification with the historical author.

The active role of the narrator in *How Far Can You Go?* means that the book contains a good deal of direct discussion of the transformations in Catholicism as well as showing them in the attitudes and behaviour of the characters. The title is first presented in a reminiscence of Michael's schooldays: 'a favourite device of the bolder spirits in the sixth form to enliven Religious Instruction was to tease the old priest who took them for this lesson with casuistical questions of sexual morality, especially the question of How Far You Could Go with the opposite sex. *"Please, Father, how far can you go with a girl, Father?"'* (*HFCYG* 4). By the end of the novel the question has a wider and less literal application; it asks how far can Catholics, or the Church, change and still retain anything identifiable as Catholic identity. Early on the narrator describes the world-picture that his young Catholics would have grown up with. It took the form of a great snakes-and-ladders board with Salvation as the name of the game; at the top was Heaven and at the bottom was Hell; prayers and sacraments and good deeds sent you scuttling up a ladder; sins sent you slithering down a snake. The rules were complicated, but anything you very much liked doing was almost certainly bad, or at least a moral danger. This account would have been regarded by thoughtful Catholics, well before Vatican II, as a caricature, since it excludes any idea of a loving Creator or an autonomous spiritual life. Nevertheless, there is no denying that something like this caricature was what cradle-Catholics often grew up with. In the novel, Lodge's characters gradually come to abandon it, not by a conscious rethinking of doctrine but by a steady change in their sense of what seemed credible. 'At some point in the 1960s', remarks the narrator, 'Hell disappeared. No one could say for certain when this happened. First it was there, then it wasn't'. By the end of the decade the married couples had all taken to using contraception, in defiance of *Humanae Vitae*. The narrator subjects the Catholic position on contraception to a chilly analysis; it was more logical, he suggests, when the Church believed, like Father Finbar in *The British Museum is Falling Down*, that the purpose of marriage was simply the procreation and education of children. But then the emphasis changed; marital sexual pleasure was regarded as acceptable, even proper (in defiance of ancient traditions), and the use of the safe period, which had been reluctantly tolerated as a means of birth control, was actively encouraged. All of which meant that the ban on contraceptive methods, based on abstruse metaphysical arguments, came to seem less and less cogent. Furthermore, the starry-eyed praise of sexual happiness – in marriage, naturally – by the new theologians meant that young Catholics were disinclined to wait patiently for marriage before enjoying it, as the characters in *How Far Can You Go?* had done. In this novel Lodge opens up an entirely new subject, and describes, with sombre wit and painfully sharp observation, a subculture on the point of meltdown.

The last chapter of the novel contains the script of a television programme, presenting a Paschal Festival put on at Easter 1975 by Catholics for an Open Church, a reformist group which includes the characters of the novel who are still practising believers. At intervals in the programme, a 'voice over' comments on the symbolic and liturgical action and its implications, and Lodge has associated this narratorial voice with his own view of the issues raised. It announces 'the fading away of the traditional Catholic metaphysic – that marvellously complex and ingenious synthesis of theology and cosmology and casuistry, which situated individual souls on a kind of spiritual Snakes and Ladders board, motivated them with equal doses of hope and fear, and promised them, if they persevered in the game, an eternal reward' (*HFCYG* 239). Within another generation or two, the speaker believes, 'it will have disappeared, superseded by something less vivid but more tolerant. Christian unity is now a feasible objective for the first time since the Reformation'. He goes on to propose a future for religion in terms which Lodge has developed elsewhere: belief involves necessary but provisional narratives with which we try to make sense of existence, and which have analogies with literary narratives:

> Just as when reading a novel, or writing one for that matter, we maintain a double consciousness of the characters as both, as it were, real and fictitious, free and determined, and know that however absorbing and convincing we may find it, it is not the only story we shall want to read (or, as the case may be, write) but part of an endless sequence of stories by which man has sought and will always seek to make sense of life. And death. (*HFCYG* 240)

But this speculation is not quite the end of the story. The author moves on a few more pages, and years, and in the final paragraph announces the election in 1978 of a new pope, a Pole and the first non-Italian for 400 years, adding 'all bets are void, the future is uncertain'. It was a prudent intervention, for John Paul II proved to be a pontiff of charismatic, conservative and authoritarian temperament, with little sympathy for modernizing liberal Catholics; he made great efforts to deflect if not reverse the thrust of Vatican II, and to undo many of the changes that stemmed from it. Right-wing and traditionalist groups in the Church revived, and the 'traditional Catholic metaphysic' did not fade away in the manner predicted in *How Far Can You Go?*. The divisions between liberals and conservatives remained in place, and argument continued. The ban on contraception was reaffirmed, but was widely disregarded.

In 1991 Lodge returned to the Catholic questions in *Paradise News*. It had a more mixed reception than his last few novels, and it is true that it is milder and gentler, without the inventiveness and displays of wit readers had come to expect. It has a retrospective quality, as he takes the opportunity, after more than thirty years of writing, to revisit the places and themes of his earlier work. The novel is partly set in Rummidge, not in its university but in a rather run-down theological college; one chapter takes us to Brickley, the South London suburb which provided the setting for *The Picturegoers*; and most of the action occurs in Hawaii, where Persse McGarrigle had briefly touched down in *Small World*. Lodge's last 'Catholic' novel raised and tried to answer the question, 'How far can you go?' In *Paradise News* the response is, 'Further still'. In the earlier novel, Father Austin Brierley has passed through many vicissitudes after his conventional beginning, has left the priesthood and married, but remains 'a kind of Catholic'. Bernard Walsh, the central figure of *Paradise News*, has gone further, for he has abandoned not only the priesthood but Catholic belief itself. He is the son of a London Irish family in Brickley, which is reminiscent of the Mallorys, but is shown in a harsher light. At the end of *The Picturegoers* Mark Underwood goes off to become a priest, to the general approbation of the Catholic characters, and, one imagines, the author. One of the Mallory sons, James, is already a priest, and another, Patrick, is expected to become one, though it is not clear how far he shares this expectation. Bernard, like the Mallorys a parishioner of Our Lady of Perpetual Succour, Brickley, enters the priesthood, not out of deep dedication and spiritual zeal, but because his family hope he will become a priest, and he is drawn to the privileges and status of the priestly life and scared of the demands of the larger world. The Mallory family had been depicted as admirable people, but the Walsh family is permeated by self-deception and bad faith. Bernard suggests what might have happened to James or Patrick in the uncertain future that followed Vatican II.

He serves as a priest to the best of his abilities, and becomes a lecturer in theology at a seminary. But his faith, never robust, is steadily dwindling, and Lodge effectively traces the intellectual and psychological process of the decline. The final break is prompted by sex, when Bernard, a 40-year-old celibate and virgin, falls, or is led, into an affair with a woman whom he is supposedly instructing in Catholicism. It ends disastrously for both of them. After he has left the priesthood, Bernard scrapes a modest living as an unbelieving part-time lecturer in theology at a college in Rummidge. Now in his mid-40s, he is a lonely and depressed figure, with few friends, and more or less alienated from his family, who have found it difficult to forgive his abandonment of the priesthood.

The plot transports Bernard from Rummidge to Hawaii. His Aunt Ursula had long ago moved to the United States, like Kate in *Out of the Shelter*, and has retired to Hawaii. She telephones Bernard, whom she has not seen for many years, to tell him that she is suffering from inoperable cancer and may not live much longer. Before she dies she wants to meet again and make her peace with her brother Jack, Bernard's father, from whom she has long been estranged. She urges Bernard to bring Jack to Hawaii, and will pay their fares. Bernard is more than ready to make the trip, but his father, a cantankerous Irish widower who lives alone in Brickley, needs a great deal of persuasion. Eventually he agrees, spurred by the hope of getting something in his sister's will. Bernard finds that a package holiday in Hawaii is much cheaper than two ordinary return air tickets, so they make the long flight as tourists. Lodge moves easily into a comic mode in his description of their fellow travellers – who include Brian Everthorpe, previously encountered in *Nice Work* – and in satirical reflections on the phenomenon of global tourism; he carefully registers the exotic appearances and *mores* of Hawaii, an American state which is in every sense halfway to the Far East. But the comic dimension of the novel is a little perfunctory. The real interest is in the story of Bernard and what happens to him in Hawaii, a gentle, painful and moving story.

Bernard does what he can to make his aunt more comfortable, and her situation makes him think steadily about death. The prayers and liturgy which he used to conduct as a priest are full of references to the world to come, where those who have lived a good life on earth can expect an eternity of happiness with God. According to the Catechism, the Christian is to love and serve God in his life, and be happy with him for ever in the next (Bernard notes sardonically that there is nothing about happiness in *this* life). Hope in heaven is still an essential part of the faith of most Christians, especially those who have found little reward in their earthly existence. But the advanced theologians whom Bernard studies and teaches are silent about an afterlife. Hell quietly disappeared for the liberal Catholics in *How Far Can You Go?*, and it seems that heaven may have gone the same way. If so, a traditional hope for humanity has been snatched away. Ordinary believers, though, may be unaware and unaffected by this shift, since theologians write not for them but for each other; there is an analogy, which Lodge has pursued elsewhere, with the way in which academic literary criticism and theory are now incomprehensible to unprofessional readers of literature.

Bernard dwells on these questions in the intervals of looking after his aunt, and his father, who is injured in a traffic accident on their first day in Hawaii. The woman driving the car which runs into Jack is very concerned about him, though entirely blameless (Jack, not used to traffic coming from the right, was looking the wrong way). She is Yolande, an attractive woman of 40, who came to Hawaii from the continental USA some years before because of her husband's academic job; now they have split up and she is seeking a divorce. After some hesitation on his part, Bernard and Yolande embark on an affair, which is both passionate and tender. He finds unfamiliar happiness and a tentative hope for the future, since their love is shared and the relationship may continue. Yolande is keen to leave Hawaii, having had more than enough of the island paradise and its supposedly perfect climate, and is intrigued by the idea of the English Midlands, despite the weather. It is a thoroughly romantic episode, but Lodge presents it very persuasively.

When he arrives at the airport in Hawaii Bernard picks up a tourist brochure called *Paradise News*, and he soon discovers that practically everything in the islands connects itself to Paradise: 'Paradise Finance Inc., Paradise Sportswear, Paradise Supply Inc., Paradise Beauty and Barber Suppliers, Paradise Beverages, Paradise Puppets, Paradise Snorkel Adventures, Paradise Tinting, Paradise Cleaning and Maintenance Service, Paradise Parking'. The insistent and ultimately meaningless repetition of the word is counter-pointed with Bernard's mingled doubts and hopes about the spiritual paradise of Christian tradition. He finds romance in Hawaii, but he is also in a Romance, of the kind that Lodge is very interested in. The image of Hawaii as an earthly paradise is a commercialized vulgarity, but he attempts to redeem the term and revive its ancient associations; in the novel, Hawaii has affinities with the magic island of *The Tempest*, which is quoted more than once, and with the Fortunate Isles of European mythology.

Back in Rummidge, Bernard receives a letter from Yolande, saying that she may marry him in time, and meanwhile wants to come to England to spend Christmas with him. A colleague asks Bernard if he has had good news, and he replies, in the final words of the novel, 'Very good news'. It is indeed, for Bernard at that point in his life; but the phrase 'good news' also referred to the Gospel and the Christian hope for the future. Bernard's experiences in Hawaii may not have restored his faith, but they have given him hope, which is a theological virtue as well as a human quality. The tentatively happy ending of *Paradise News* emphasises its affinities with the Romance mode rather than with the despairing realism of much modern fiction. Lodge's use of the semi-magic plot devices of the Victorian novel is continued from *Nice Work*; there an unexpected legacy arrives from Australia, and in *Paradise News* an overlooked share certificate among Ursula's modest assets proves to have become immensely valuable, enabling her to spend her final weeks in dignity and comfort; and, after her death, to benefit Bernard's sister, who is coping with a brain-damaged child. (He refuses any share in the money.)

In *How Far Can You Go?* and *Paradise News* Lodge considers Catholicism in England during the long aftermath of the Vatican Council. Both novels show his keen if sceptical interest in religious questions, and his reading in modern theology. His personal attitude is not altogether apparent, though it is evident that he has come a long way from the kind of traditional Catholicism which underlay *The Picturegoers*; he has said of *How Far Can You Go?*: 'it brought me in a way to the edges of belief, I would say, writing that novel. I would like to think that as a result I have in some ways a more honest and profound but also a more provisional and metaphorical religious belief now than I had before...' (Walsh, 5). In 1992, Lodge attempted to define his position further. Graham Greene, one of his early models, described himself, after he had moved on from the tormented orthodoxy of his Catholic novels, as a 'Catholic agnostic'; Lodge prefers to reverse the term and call himself an 'agnostic Catholic'. He remains a practising member of the Church, though he is agnostic about the ultimate reality behind the symbolic and metaphorical languages of liturgy and scripture. Although he has abandoned much of what he has called the 'Catholic metaphysic', he insists that religious language is meaningful, as the perennial symbolic and speculative mode in which we articulate the contradictions and anxieties and hopes which are central to the human condition. Lodge acknowledges that by traditional standards, including those that he professed as a young man, he is probably a heretic; but he believes that many theologians, including Catholic ones, would now hold similar views. His position has affinities with that of the Catholic Modernists of the early twentieth century; and, less certainly, with recent radical Protestant theology. That approach, though, regards divinity as entirely immanent, whereas Lodge finds the idea of transcendence necessary to make sense of existence. Responding to the theme explored in *Paradise News*, he thinks that without some idea of life beyond death there is no point in religion, though the problem is to find an adequate language for that idea (Bergonzi 2, 71–2).

It is for theological experts to decide how far Lodge has in fact gone in moving away from the Catholic mind-set. There is, however, one important respect in which his fiction continues to reflect it, though perhaps for temperamental as much as doctrinal reasons. This has been described by Peter Widdowson:

> Lodge's Catholicism – explored historically in *How Far Can You Go?* – underpins his acceptance of bourgeois marriage as the domain in which people, whatever their frustrations and aspirations need finally to secure themselves: the family is the still point in a world turning ever faster, and the wife (usually) the one woman who has to stand in for... all the other women theoretically available in the world of sexual permissiveness. In Lodge's novels, there is always a crucial return (or *nostos*) for the main characters from the wide-open spaces, the fleshpots, the global campus, to a marriage which has to be remade. (Widdowson, 22)

Widdowson's phrase 'bourgeois marriage' indicates his own ideological agenda, but his point is valid. The marriage of Philip and Hilary Swallow has dwindled into a rather empty relationship; but they come together after the infidelities in *Changing Places*, and again in *Small World* after Philip's affair with Joy, an attractive widow with whom he had spent a night some years before, and, unknown to him, conceived a child. The revived relationship between Philip and Joy has a lot going for it, and is described in very lyrical language. Indeed, Philip wishes to marry Joy, and is on the point of asking Hilary for a divorce when she disconcerts him by telling him that she has got a job as a marriage counsellor, and he cannot bring himself to say anything. The affair comes to an end when Philip is attending a conference in Israel, with Joy in tow. He falls ill with what is at first wrongly diagnosed as Legionnaires' Disease. Panic-stricken, he asks Joy to phone Hilary, who flies out to take him home, like a mother rescuing a naughty boy in trouble. Later, Philip says of himself, 'Basically I failed in the role of romantic hero. I thought I wasn't too old for it, but I was' (*SW* 336). Meanwhile, Joy is to marry someone else. There is a hint of authorial intervention about this episode, a suggestion of a moral story in favour of the indissolubility of marriage. The Swallow marriage, according to hints in *Nice Work*, does not get any happier, but it endures after a fashion. Hilary, in her new professional role, restores the broken marriage of Swallow's former colleague, Dempsey. Admittedly, the end of *Small World* is, as I have remarked, something of a Shakespearean tableau, where broken marriages are restored and new ones made.

Already, though, in the generally graver and more realistic *How Far Can You Go?* we have seen a similar pattern. Dennis has a brief headlong affair with a much younger woman, Lynn, who thinks she is in love with him; he leaves his family and moves in with her, but after a few weeks of discomfort and sexual exhaustion he goes back to them. Eventually, she marries the ex-priest, Austin Brierley. Again, in *Nice Work*, Vic Wilcox, after his infatuation with Robyn, settles back into what has been established as a pretty unsatisfactory marriage. It is true that he would never have got anywhere with Robyn, but he need not have gone back to the dim and lymphatic Marjorie, though it is suggested that her character might improve once she has a part-time job as a secretary. The underlying assumption seems to be, adapting a remark by Samuel Johnson, that though marriage has many pains, infidelity brings no pleasure.

In his latest novel, *Therapy*, Lodge gives a significant twist to this belief. The main character, Tubby Passmore, a successful television scriptwriter, has been married, happily as he thinks, for thirty years, and he and his wife have been faithful to each other all that time (though he has a girl-friend with whom his relations are quasi-platonic and strictly non-penetrative). He takes great satisfaction at the success of his marriage, when others all around are coming apart, so he is shattered when his wife tells him that she is leaving him; not for someone else, but because she cannot stand him any more. The apparent success of his marriage was based, he discovers (as do the readers), on solipsistic complacency. In his late 50s he starts making desperate and comically unsuccessful efforts to catch up on the sexual opportunities he has long denied himself. In time he rediscovers Maureen, his first love from forty years before; she is the same age as Tubby, long married, has suffered from cancer and lost a son, and no longer has sex with her husband. Tubby falls in love with her again and begs her to marry him after they have divorced their spouses, but she is a Catholic, as she was when Tubby first knew her – when they meet up again she is making a pilgrimage to the shrine of St James at Santiago in Spain – and so is her husband. Their marriage may be sexless, she tells Tubby, but it is not loveless, and as a Catholic she will not consider divorce. Nevertheless, her conscience is accommodating enough to let her sleep with Tubby from time to time. He and Maureen and her husband, we are told on the last page, are all very great friends; it reads like another version of the fairy-tale ending.

Lodge's treatment of traditional Catholic practices is more sympathetic than in *How Far Can You Go?* or *Paradise News*, particularly in the presentation of Maureen's devotion to St James of Compostella; she knows that there is far more myth than history in his cult, but she still finds spiritual value in it. Notwithstanding his generally sceptical state of mind, Lodge responds warmly to ritual and ceremony, as ways of bringing people together for a higher end, transcending their individuality for a time. This is evident in his account of the devotions in the great Cathedral of Santiago at the end of the pilgrimage; earlier instances include the Paschal Festival in *How Far Can You Go?*, and the Hawaiian Folk Mass in *Paradise News*, which is celebrated on the beach for Ursula after her death, and which impresses the unbelieving Yolande.

Widdowson claims that Lodge's emphasis on marriage and stability, even a dull stability, 'runs counter to the openness and freedom of the novels' "Romance" rhetoric'. This is a fair comment, and the tension between romance and realism does give Lodge's more recent fiction its particular flavour. Widdowson suggests that he unfairly favours 'realism', such as carrying on with a humdrum marriage, against 'romance', which is getting a divorce and making a fresh start. But the more common mode of Romance in the novels is not the Ariostan, which is open-ended, indeed, never-ending, and involves constant fresh adventures. There is also the Shakespearean, which ends firmly, with marriages and ceremony. It first prompted Lodge's interest in Romance when, as an undergraduate, he made a special study of the late plays, with their patterns of reconciliation and transcendence. It is worth noting, too, that he wanted to end his television adaptation of Dickens's *Martin Chuzzlewit* with multiple marriages but was overruled by the director. (See Lodge's article, 'Three Weddings and a Big Row', *Independent*, 13 December 1994, which prints his intended version of the conclusion of the script.)

Unlike many modern novelists who like to humiliate and torment their characters, Lodge treats his creations with respect and affection, even at the risk of being sentimental. He is much concerned with what he calls 'providential plotting', and the happy endings of his recent novels, so against the grain of the age, emphasize the centrality of hope as a virtue, which was made explicit in *Paradise News*. Traditionally, religious literature implied a work with a happy ending, a *commedia*. Despite his agnosticism about doctrinal definitions, it makes sense to regard Lodge as a kind of religious writer.

4

Literary Criticism

During the course of his career Lodge has published several books of literary criticism and many reviews and articles. Most of his criticism is concerned with fiction, and often reflects his own interests and preoccupations as a novelist. The combination of poet and critic is familiar in literary history; the creative and critical faculties are closely related in the process of composition, since this involves not only inspiration but the capacity to test and assess what has been written, to revise and if necessary to delete. Novelists have less often been active critics, perhaps because their art is so demanding of time and effort. But Henry James, who used to rewrite other people's novels in his head when he was reading them, was a good critic, as were Virginia Woolf and E. M. Forster. And so is Lodge. He has often written as a literary journalist, with a general educated readership in mind. For many years, however, he was also a university teacher and produced the kind of academic criticism which attempts to be systematic, is specialized in its approach and terminology, and is directed in the first instance at other professionals. (Though even when writing in an academic context Lodge has usually retained the lucidity of his journalistic prose.)

His first critical book, *Language of Fiction* (1966), was published at a time when criticism of the novel was still undeveloped compared with what became known in the 1940s as the 'New Criticism', which extended and systematized the work of T. S. Eliot, I. A. Richards and William Empson in the close reading of poetry. In the 1960s serious discussion of the novel as a literary form had not developed much beyond the pioneering work of James, Forster and Percy Lubbock earlier in the century. *Language of Fiction* is essentially an attempt to apply the New Criticism to the reading of novels; its underlying assumption is that a novel is just as much a unique order of words as a poem, and has to be approached by a close analytical attention to its language. The first part of the book contains a series of succinct but inconclusive discussions of current ideas about the relations between literature and language, drawn from linguistics as well as literary scholarship. This section now looks dated and inadequate; as Lodge later pointed out, it was written before he knew anything about the relevant work of Continental structuralism.

In contrast, the practical criticism in the latter part of the book remains very useful. Here Lodge examines novels by Jane Austen, Charlotte Brontë, Dickens, Hardy, James and Wells – authors he would return to in his subsequent criticism – and concludes with a more general essay on his contemporary, Kingsley Amis. *Language of Fiction* exemplifies the New Criticism in that it pays close attention to 'the words on the page' and endeavours to see the macrocosm of the whole text implicit in the microcosm of selected passages. Lodge's approach is, in fact, less closely tied to the absolute specificity of the words than were New Critical readings of poetry; much of his analysis would, I think, work quite well with novels in translation; at least, from languages which were lexically and syntactically not too remote from English. His readings also recall the 'spatial' approach to Shakespeare, as practised by Wilson Knight and others, where key images and motifs are traced throughout a play. The whole section shows Lodge's notable acuity and tact as a close reader of fictional prose, a capacity which is intuitive as much as systematic, and which remained the principal strength of his criticism, even when he turned to different approaches. His readings in *Language of Fiction* are not of the kind we engage in on our first encounter with a novel, when we are possessed by the need to know what happens next; but they resemble the process of rereading, when we know what has happened and is to come, and can think of the whole text as spread out before us (and can refresh our memories by turning the pages back and forth).

Here and there the accents of the practitioner are heard in *Language of Fiction*, as when Lodge prefaces his analysis of a famous episode in James's *The Ambassadors* with the remark, 'My argument keeps returning to the scene on the river, and I should confess that it began with a wish to account for my enormous admiration for the way that scene is done' (*LF* 194). This is the tone of a young artist admiring the skill of a master. His interest in 'the way things are

49

done' means that Lodge's criticism tends to be formalist, rather than ethical in the influential line of Matthew Arnold and F. R. Leavis. He has discussed the distinction, invoking the terms 'Aristotelian' and 'Platonic' and defending his own 'Aristotelian' position, in an interesting review of Laurence Lerner's *The Truthtellers* (*NAC* 49). In addition to his bias as a practitioner, Lodge's Catholic background and education may have made him unresponsive to the Arnoldian assumption that literature can, in effect, function as a mode of religion. At the same time, he avoids the extremes of an inhuman aestheticism or of a narrowly technical approach to literary questions. He writes, 'In the last analysis, criticism claims our attention, not as sets of data nor as sets of conclusions, but as human discourse' (*LF* 87). This attitude is familiar in English cultural debate, and certainly in line with Lodge's temperamental attitudes; he retreated from it somewhat in the 1970s under the influence of structuralism, but returned to it in the 1980s, after he had discovered Mikhail Bakhtin.

Lodge's next book of criticism, *The Novelist at the Crossroads* (1971) was a collection of essays, some of them general studies of recent fiction and criticism; others were concerned with particular authors, including his fellow Catholics, Chesterton, Belloc, Graham Greene and Muriel Spark; and Americans such as Hemingway, William Burroughs and John Updike. The long title essay looks at the state of the English and American novel in the late 1960s. The crossroads where Lodge located the novelist pointed in a number of directions: towards the broad highway of traditional realism; towards myth, fantasy, fabulation (and, to use a term not yet current, 'magic realism'); towards the 'non-fiction novel', where a work of journalism or history or biography draws on the rhetorical and narrative devices of the novel; and towards the self-aware or problematical novel, later called 'metafiction', in which the problems of sustaining a narrative are part of the story; as in *Tristram Shandy*, and many modern instances, including some by Lodge himself. Commenting on this essay in 1992, he wrote, 'the aesthetic pluralism I sought to defend in my "Novelist at the Crossroads" essay seems to be now a generally accepted fact of literary life... The astonishing variety of styles on offer today, as if in an aesthetic supermarket, includes traditional as well as innovative styles, minimalism as well as excess, nostalgia as well as prophecy' (*NT* 209).

In his original essay Lodge looks tolerantly at the different possibilities open to the novelist, whilst himself remaining committed to traditional realism, which he defends with Johnsonian directness: 'while many aspects of contemporary experience encourage an extreme apocalyptic response, most of us continue to live our lives on the assumption that the reality which realism imitates actually exists. History may be, in a philosophical sense, a fiction, but it does not feel like that when we miss a train or somebody starts a war' (*NAC* 33). This was a position which Lodge continued to adhere to, emotionally if not altogether intellectually, and which underlay his novels, even in the metafictional devices of *How Far Can You Go?* and *Small World.* However, his interest in structuralism made him wary about what Roland Barthes called 'the classic realist text'; in 1984 he observed, 'the metafictional apparatus of *How Far Can You Go?* questions the realistic convention at the same time as the book is using that convention' (Haffenden, 157).

By the late 1960s academic critics had come to feel that the familiar modes of reading literature, whether New Critical or Leavisite, scholarly or aesthetic, were becoming exhausted and that new approaches were needed. As a result there was a turn to the structuralism which had been dominant for some time in French intellectual life, and an enthusiastic if not always well-informed attempt to learn from it and perhaps to assimilate it to Anglophone methods. Lodge shared this interest; he spent much of the 1970s studying structuralist criticism, especially of narrative, and the results are evident in his next books of criticism: *The Modes of Modern Writing* (1977) and *Working with Structuralism* (1981). In his Preface to the latter, Lodge writes, 'Nobody professionally involved in the world of literary scholarship in England or America can deny that the most striking development of the last twenty years has been this massive swing of attention towards Continental structuralism' (*WS* vii). He describes structuralism as having two branches:

> One is the extension of what I would call classical structuralism. It is concerned with the analysis and understanding of culture as a series of systems, of which language is usually taken as the ideal model for explanatory purposes. This structuralism aims to do for literature – or myth, or food or fashion – what grammar does for language: to understand and explain how these systems work, what are the rules and

constraints within which, and by virtue of which, meaning is generated and communicated. It is essentially formalist and aspires to the status of science. The second branch of structuralism, perhaps more properly called poststructuralism, is ideological in orientation. It combines the anti-empirical methodology of classical structuralism with ideas derived from Marxism, psychoanalysis and philosophy, to analyse cultural institutions, such as literature, as mediations of ideologies. This structuralism is polemical and *engagé*. Jakobson, Lévi-Strauss, and Todorov would be representative figures of the first branch of structuralism; Foucault, Lacan and Derrida of the second. (*WS* ix)

Lodge makes it clear that his allegiance is to the former or 'classical' mode. Even as he wrote, though, the second, poststructuralist mode – which was more various and contradictory than his summary might suggest – was moving rapidly into academic dominance in America, and was becoming fashionable among young English academics, like Robyn and Charles in *Nice Work*. *The Modes of Modern Writing* is Lodge's most systematic and theoretically ambitious critical work. Its point of departure is the distinction developed by the Russian linguistician Roman Jakobson between 'metaphor' and 'metonymy', which he claimed was of central importance in literary discourse and in many other kinds of cultural activity. Structuralist analysis was often based on binary oppositions, and these were imaginatively congenial to Lodge, as we see in several of his novels.

A few years earlier he had doubted the possibility of discovering a comprehensive 'poetics of fiction', but he came to see it as a necessary task for the critical theorist. Two quotations show the shift: 'I am certainly sceptical of the possibilities of formulating a poetics of the novel analogous to that which Aristotle formulated for the tragic drama of his time . . .'; 'What is needed is a single way of talking about novels, a critical methodology, a poetics or aesthetics of fiction, which can embrace descriptively all the varieties of this way of writing' (*NAC* 54; *MMW* 52). I am not scoring points over Lodge's inconsistency; the real interest is in tracing his determined successive attempts to gain a theoretical understanding of the art which he practised with such accomplishment, attempts which led him on an intellectual progress from the New Criticism to structuralism to Bakhtin; for a time he allowed the system-making enthusiasms of structuralism to overcome his cautious scepticism about large enterprises.

The Modes of Modern Writing is an attempt to interpret the history of twentieth-century literature in terms of the metaphor/ metonymy distinction. Metaphor relates things in terms of their resemblances, and metonymy in terms of contiguity and association; the latter figure is close to synecdoche, where the whole is taken for the part, or vice versa (as in 'Whitehall' for a government department, or 'hands' for factory workers). Lodge illustrates the difference by rewriting the sentence 'ships sailed the sea' as 'keels ploughed the deep'. 'Keels' where a part of the ship is taken for the whole, is synecdoche; 'ploughed' is a metaphor for 'sailed'; and 'the deep', a quality associated with the seas, is metonymy ('the briny' would have been an alternative). In *Nice Work* Robyn expounds the distinction to a baffled Vic Wilcox in terms of cigarette advertisements: Silk Cut is metaphoric, Marlboro metonymic. Presented in such simple terms, the distinction makes sense, and some of Lodge's applications of it are revealing; traditionally realistic writing tends to be metonymic, and modernist writing tends to be metaphoric. But the absolute nature of the distinction is elusive. One of the chapters of *The Modes of Modern Writing* is called 'The Metaphoric and Metonymic Poles', but it is evident that we are not concerned with a fundamental binary opposition, of the kind that underlies computer technology, for instance. Lodge himself says as much: 'we are not discussing a distinction between two mutually exclusive types of discourse, but a distinction based on dominance. The metaphoric work cannot totally neglect metonymic continuity if it is to be intelligible at all. Correspondingly, the metonymic text cannot eliminate all signs that it is available for metaphorical interpretation' (*MMW* 111). The concept of 'dominance' is taken from the linguistics of the Prague School, but it has its own uncertainties. Ninety per cent can be interpreted as dominance, but what of fifty-one per cent? Literary texts are inevitably mixed affairs; the metaphor/metonymy distinction is comprehensible as a kind of laboratory model, but, in the process of reading, the terms can be hard to keep apart; for instance, Lodge says of a passage from Hemingway that 'an apparently metonymic style is made to serve the purpose of metaphor' (*MMW* 159). The theoretical framework is shaky, but *The Modes of Modern Writing* throws out many interesting ideas. As with

Language of Fiction, the major value of the book lies in Lodge's discussion of specific works and authors, where the metaphor/ metonymy distinction is at best an approximate guide. The essay on Joyce, which moves in a few pages of lucid exposition from an early story, 'The Sisters', to *Finnegans Wake*, is masterly, and would make an ideal introduction to Joyce's work.

Working with Structuralism is a collection of essays, only a handful of which show clearly structuralist leanings. Lodge suggests in his Preface that structuralism had become such a dominant intellectual presence that one had to work with or alongside it, whatever one thought about it. This is a little reminiscent of those collaborationists in the Second World War who were convinced of the victory of the Third Reich and resigned themselves to 'working with the Germans'. Lodge himself said the book might have been called 'Living with Structuralism', which reminded a reviewer of 'surviving with sciatica'. The first essay – originally Lodge's inaugural lecture as Professor of Modern English Literature at Birmingham – reproduces some of the arguments of *The Modes of Modern Writing* and falls into a common confusion about Ferdinand de Saussure's distinction between 'signifier' and 'signified' (for discussion of this confusion, see Scholes, 1985 and Tallis, 1988). Under Saussure's influence Lodge draws the very dubious conclusion that the great modernist texts had no necessary connection with 'reality'. (The London of *The Waste Land*, the Dublin of *Ulysses*?) This is an odd claim for a keen-eyed writer of avowedly realistic novels, and Lodge never advanced it again. *Working with Structuralism* contains narratological analyses of a story by Hemingway and one by Lodge himself, which are interesting as demonstrations of a method, but are remote from the normal process of reading. In his Preface he unashamedly admits his eclecticism, and most of the essays are in the modes that he is more evidently at ease with, where close reading is reinforced by knowledge, when appropriate, of biographical and historical contexts. There are three essays on Hardy, and two on Evelyn Waugh; in one of the best pieces, 'Ambiguously Ever After', Lodge writes as a practitioner about the problems of ending a novel, and discusses the way in which some novels have had more than one conclusion. In the last part of the collection he moves from purely literary questions to aspects of popular culture, as he interprets Ted Hughes's *Crow* as a cartoon figure, assesses the New Journalism of Tom Wolfe, and is fascinated by the psychobabble of Californian yuppies.

In the 1970s it was fashionable to describe many kinds of cultural activity as a 'language'. Lodge more than once claimed that narrative was itself a language, with a grammar. Nevertheless, the term is no more than a loose, suggestive metaphor. Two competent users of a language with an understanding of its grammar would certainly agree on the structure of a sentence in that language; but I doubt that two narratologists would ever be in such complete agreement about the structure of a short story, let alone a whole novel. Umberto Eco has made a relevant caveat: 'The "grammar" of traffic lights and the structure of a phonological system seem to be more "objective" (more "scientific") than the description of the narrative function in Russian fairy tales; and the narrative function of the Russian fairy tales seems to be less questionable than, let us say, a possible system of narrative function in the novels of French Romanticism' (Eco 5). Lodge learnt from the studies in narrative of Genette and Todorov, but in general the hopes raised by classical structuralism were not fulfilled; before long it was displaced by poststructuralism, for which he had little sympathy.

Lodge found a way forward in his theoretical thinking about literature in the work of Mikhail Bakhtin, who died in obscurity in Russia in 1975, but made a substantial posthumous impact on western literary scholarship. The structuralist enterprise was conducted at some remove from imaginative literature, since its points of reference were in linguistics, anthropology and philosophy; Bakhtin, however, drew his method from the close study of two great writers, Rabelais and Dostoevsky. He was primarily interested in fiction, and in the notion of 'dialogue', which he sees as central to the novel, as opposed to the monologism of older modes such as epic and lyric. For Bakhtin human discourse is part of a continuing process, where words imply other words already spoken, and others yet to be uttered, in continuation, agreement or rebuttal. Among his key terms are 'polyphony' and 'heteroglossia', both implying a multiplicity of voices.

The discovery of these ideas was very fruitful for Lodge, as he describes in the Introduction to *After Bakhtin* (1990). He acknowledges that *The Modes of Modern Writing* was 'not entirely free from the tendency of most stylistic criticism to treat the language of a novel as if it were a homogeneous entity'. Such criticism cannot adequately cope with fictional dialogue; but this, adds Lodge, is where Bakhtin comes in, 'explaining that there is no such thing as *the* style, *the* language of a novel, because a novel is a medley of many styles, many languages – or, if you like, many voices' (*AB* 6). Bakhtin freed Lodge from the unrewarding attempt to find monistic explanations, and brought his critical speculations back towards his instincts as a practising novelist; he responded warmly to Bakhtin's remark, 'For the prose artist the world is full of other people's words, among which he must orient himself and whose speech characteristics he must be able to perceive with a very keen ear' (*AB* 7). *After Bakhtin* is a collection of essays linked by Bakhtinian insights, mainly on nineteenth- and twentieth-century novelists, and it contains some of Lodge's best critical writing. 'Mimesis and Diegesis in Modern Fiction' is particularly impressive, going back to the terms in Plato which provided the basis for Bakhtin's distinction between monologue and dialogue (which in turn has affinities with James's 'showing' and 'telling'), and acutely applying them to a range of modern novels. The book appeared not long after Lodge had given up working in a university, and in his Introduction he reflects dryly on the current state of academic criticism:

A vast amount of it is not, like the work of Bakhtin, a contribution to human knowledge, but the demonstration of a professional mastery by translating known facts into more and more arcane metalanguages. This is not an entirely pointless activity – it sharpens the wits and tests the stamina of those who produce and consume such work – but it seems less and less relevant to my own writing practice. Though I intend to go on writing literary criticism, I doubt whether it will be 'academic' in the way most of the essays included in this book are academic. If the title *After Bakhtin* has a faintly elegiac ring, then, that is not entirely inappropriate. (*AB* 8)

Lodge's next work of criticism was indeed very different. *The Art of Fiction* (1992) contains short informal articles written for a series in a Sunday newspaper. He discusses the technical and thematic devices and resources of fiction, drawing on his own practice as a novelist and his long experience as a literary critic. Lodge takes examples of how the art of fiction works from many of the canonical writers he has discussed in the past – Austen,

Dickens, George Eliot, Hardy, James, Greene, and Waugh, among others – and from a variety of contemporary novelists, British and American. The book is directed at a non-professional audience of novel readers (and, no doubt, of potential novel writers), whom Lodge evidently found rewarding to write for, and who would have certainly learnt a lot from it. The academic critic has reverted to the ancient and honourable role of the man of letters.

5

Lodge and the Art of Fiction

Lodge has described how writing sketches for a stage revue helped to turn him into a comic novelist, and he has kept in touch with the medium of drama. In 1991 his play *The Writing Game*, a farce set in a residential school of creative writing, was performed at the Birmingham Rep. It is television, though, that has offered him the greatest opportunities as a dramatic writer. In 1989 he adapted *Nice Work* as a television serial, and he has described the experience and the lessons he learnt from it in an essay, 'Adapting *Nice Work* for Television' (*ANWT*). Then in 1994 his adaptation of Dickens's *Martin Chuzzlewit* was broadcast by BBC2 and highly praised.

Television provided Lodge with the material and the milieu for his tenth novel, *Therapy* (1995), one of whose epigraphs is a remark by Graham Greene to the effect that writing is a form of therapy. The central figure and narrator, Tubby Passmore, is a very successful scriptwriter whose world suddenly falls apart when his wife leaves him. He is depressed, even shattered, but manages to survive. Tubby resembles the middle-aged heroes of many American novels, who undergo all kinds of personal, professional and sexual disasters, but who remain fiercely articulate and opinionated in the midst of everything; an English cousin of Saul Bellow's Moses Herzog, perhaps. Lodge has found a stimulating new setting in *Therapy*, the competitive, bitchy, insecure, but energetic and energizing world of television, and he extracts splendid comedy from it. The new material is expressed in a new fictional form; he has long regarded each novel he embarks on as presenting a fresh set of formal problems to be encountered and solved. *Therapy* is Lodge's first novel since *Ginger, You're Barmy* to be told entirely in the first person, though

58

with a significant difference. The earlier novel was supposed to be a written narrative (as were the extracts from Bernard Walsh's journal in *Paradise News*) but Tubby's narrative is a *spoken* utterance, colloquial, slangy, sometimes obscene, registering every shift of mood from exasperation to exaltation. This kind of oral monologue was called *skaz* by the Russian Formalist critics, and it has been a conspicuous element of American novels since Mark Twain; one thinks of J. D. Salinger, of Bellow (though *Herzog* is told in the third person), of Norman Mailer, of Joseph Heller. Lodge has commented, 'First person narration appeals to contemporary novelists because it permits the writer to remain within the conventions of realism without claiming the kind of authority which belongs to the authorial narrative method of the classic realist novel' (*NT* 209). The fact that *Therapy* is a monologue may seem to go against Lodge's regard for Bakhtin and the dialogic principle, but Tubby's utterance, assertive but insecure, pleading or argumentative, is always aware of other voices that have to be answered or placated. And at the heart of the book is a *tour de force* of writing in which the monologue becomes ventriloquial or heteroglossic.

Tubby is an intelligent but undereducated man, with a marked intellectual curiosity, somewhat reminiscent of Joyce's Leopold Bloom. In the midst of his personal crisis he develops a passionate interest in the nineteenth-century Danish philosopher and theologian, Kierkegaard; finding, as he puts it, that he could not resist a thinker who wrote books with such titles as *Fear and Trembling*, *The Concept of Dread*, and *Sickness Unto Death*. Tubby invokes and takes to heart a dictum of Kierkegaard's: 'The most dreadful thing that can happen to a man is to become ridiculous in a matter of essential importance'. The iconoclastic Lutheran, Kierkegaard, and his home town of Copenhagen, where Tubby goes on a private pilgrimage, provide one pole of a North–South, Protestant–Catholic opposition; the other is St James and the city of Santiago, which Tubby discovers when he gets caught up in a public pilgrimage as he seeks his Catholic first love, Maureen. But *Therapy* is anything but schematic; the genial comedy arises out of its serious qualities.

A concern with form is central to Lodge's sense of his responsibilities as a novelist, and of his interests as a critic. His idea of the comic concerns the shape of a novel, as well as involving comic episodes and speeches. The well-absorbed influence of Joyce is always apparent, in the matter of comic form, in the precise placing of every word, and in a keen responsiveness to the sounds of the words. Lodge expresses a central modernist conviction in resisting any separation between form and content. This sets him in opposition to those writers and critics who, for ideological reasons, regard 'content' as of primary importance. It is true that in his structuralist phase Lodge sometimes inclined to give the priority to 'form', but in general he has refused to separate them. It is appropriate that he called his latest critical book *The Art of Fiction*, acknowledging that it trespassed on the title of a magisterial essay by Henry James. Lodge admires James, and would no doubt be happy to echo the sentiment that James expressed during his quarrel with Wells about the nature of fiction: 'It is art that *makes* life, makes interest, makes importance'. In a successful work of literary art it is form that delivers content, and makes it accessible.

Lodge is unusual and fortunate in being a best-selling novelist of wide appeal who nevertheless takes the art of fiction very seriously, often writes intertextually and allusively, and is willing to challenge his readers as well as entertain them. A concern with art is sometimes thought of as leading to preciosity, to triviality and empty aestheticism; if it does that, it is a distortion, and it is not one that Lodge has ever been drawn to. As a comic novelist in a mainstream of English writing that goes back to Fielding and beyond, he is constantly fascinated by the absurdity and untidiness of the human lot. He is interested, too, in ideas about how civilization is maintained; in his novels comedy is interwoven with serious reflections on religion and society, literature and education. Lodge summed up his sense of personal and artistic responsibility to an interviewer in 1993:

> Sometimes, in relation to the academic novels, I'm described as being rather cruelly satirical. I don't think of myself as a cruel writer. I am generous sometimes to the point of sentimentality and I think that's a weakness I have to watch. When you're writing novels you are in a sort of God-like position, because you are dispensing fortune, you are putting characters into jeopardy, into situations of conflict, and you can reward them or punish them. And whatever you do is going to betray something of what you think life is like or what you hope it could be like. I'm certainly reluctant to put my characters through really harrowing experiences.
>
> My novels are comic, not only in the sense of being funny, but also

in structure. The patterns of comedy, and romantic comedy in older literature, always attracted me and fascinated me. I was always very interested in Shakespeare's romances and late plays for instance. I suppose this comes out in my novels. They're either open-ended, deliberately unresolved, or else they're rather optimistic. Although I can read and enjoy very different kinds of writing – total negativity and despair, as in Beckett – I could not possibly write like that. It is completely foreign to me. (Kostrzewa, 10)

Select Bibliography

WORKS BY DAVID LODGE

Books and Pamphlets

About Catholic Authors (London, 1958).

Introducing Jazz (by D.J.L.) (London, 1959).

The Picturegoers (London, 1960; 2nd edn. with introduction, Harmondsworth, 1993).

Ginger, You're Barmy (London, 1962; New York, 1965; 2nd edn. with afterword, London, 1982).

The British Museum is Falling Down (London, 1965; New York, 1967; 2nd edn. with introduction, London, 1981).

Graham Greene (New York, 1966).

Language of Fiction: Essays in Criticism and Verbal Analysis of the English Novel (London and New York, 1966; 2nd edn. with afterword, London, 1984).

Out of the Shelter (London, 1970; 2nd edn. revised with introduction, London, 1985; New York, 1989).

The Novelist at the Crossroads and Other Essays on Fiction and Criticism (London and Ithaca, 1971).

Evelyn Waugh (New York, 1971).

Changing Places: A Tale of Two Campuses (London, 1975; New York, 1978).

The Modes of Modern Writing: Metaphor, Metonymy, and the Typology of Modern Literature (London and Ithaca, 1977).

Modernism, Antimodernism and Postmodernism (Birmingham, 1977).

How Far Can You Go? (London, 1980; as *Souls and Bodies*, New York, 1982).

Working with Structuralism: Essays and Reviews on Nineteenth and Twentieth Century Literature (London, 1981).

Small World: An Academic Romance (London, 1984; New York, 1985).

Write On: Occasional Essays '65–'85 (London, 1986).

Nice Work (London, 1988; New York, 1989).

After Bakhtin: Essays on Fiction and Criticism (London and New York, 1990).

Paradise News (London and New York, 1991).

The Writing Game: A Comedy (London, 1991).

The Art of Fiction (London and New York, 1992).

A David Lodge Trilogy (Harmondsworth, 1993). Contains *Changing Places, Small World* and *Nice Work*.

Three Novels (London, 1994). Contains *Ginger, You're Barmy, The British Museum is Falling Down* and *How Far Can You Go?*

Therapy: A Novel (London and New York, 1995).

Short Stories

'The Man Who Couldn't Get Up', *Weekend Telegraph*, 6 May 1966.

'My First Job', *London Review of Books*, 4 September 1980.

'Where the Climate's Sultry', *Cosmopolitan*, August 1987.

'Hotel des Boobs', in *The Penguin Book of Modern British Short Stories*, ed. M. Bradbury (London, 1988; New York, 1989).

'Pastoral', in *Telling Stories*, ed. D. Minshull (London, 1992).

Uncollected Essays

'Pay As You Learn', *Listener*, 5 October 1989.

'Fact and Fiction in the Novel: An Author's Note', in *Tensions and Transitions (1869–1990): The Mediating Imagination*, ed. M. Irwin, M. Kinkead-Weekes and A.R. Lee (London, 1990).

'The Novelist Today: Still at the Crossroads?', in *New Writing*, ed. M. Bradbury and J. Cooke (London, 1992).

'Adapting *Nice Work* for Television', in *Novel Images: Literature in Performance*, ed. P. Reynolds (London and New York, 1993).

'Three Weddings and a Big Row' (on Lodge's television adaptation of *Martin Chuzzlewit*), *Independent*, 13 December 1994.

Edited Works and Introductions

Jane Austen: 'Emma', A Macmillan Casebook (London, 1968).
Jane Austen, *Emma*, with James Kinsley (London, 1971).
Twentieth Century Literary Criticism: A Reader (London, 1972).
George Eliot, *Scenes of Clerical Life* (Harmondsworth, 1973).
Thomas Hardy, *The Woodlanders* (London, 1974).
The Best of Ring Lardner (London, 1984).
François Mauriac, *Knot of Vipers* (Harmondsworth, 1985).
Henry James, *The Spoils of Poynton* (Harmondsworth, 1987).
Modern Criticism and Theory: A Reader (London, 1988).
Kingsley Amis, *Lucky Jim* (Harmondsworth, 1992).

INTERVIEWS WITH DAVID LODGE

Bergonzi, B., 'David Lodge Interviewed', *The Month* (February, 1970), 108–16.
_____ 'A Religious Romance: David Lodge in Conversation', *The Critic* (Fall, 1992), 68–73.
Haffenden, J., 'David Lodge', in *Novelists in Interview* (London, 1985).
Kostrzewa, R., 'The Novel and Its Enemies: A Conversation with David Lodge', *Harkness Report* (December, 1993), 8–11.
Walsh, C., 'David Lodge Interviewed', *Strawberry Fare* (Autumn, 1984), 3–12.

CRITICAL AND BIOGRAPHICAL STUDIES

Bergonzi, B., *The Myth of Modernism and Twentieth Century Literature* (Brighton, 1986). Contains 'The Decline and Fall of the Catholic Novel', an essay relating Lodge to earlier Catholic novelists.
_____ *Exploding English: Criticism, Theory, Culture* (Oxford, 1990). Discusses Lodge's criticism and fiction in a critique of academic English study.
Bradbury, M., and D. Palmer (eds), *The Contemporary English Novel* (London, 1979). Contains Robert Burden's 'The Novel Interrogates Itself', which discusses *The British Museum is Falling Down*.

Halio, J. L. (ed.), *British Novelists Since 1960* (Detroit, 1983).

Honan, P., 'David Lodge and the Cinematic Novel in England', *Novel* (Winter, 1972), 167–73. On Lodge's early novels.

Morace, R.A., *The Dialogic Novels of Malcolm Bradbury and David Lodge* (Carbondale, 1989).

Moseley, M., *David Lodge: How Far Can You Go?* (San Bernandino, 1991). A lucid survey of Lodge's work up to 1988.

Parnell, M., 'The Novels of David Lodge', *Madog* (Summer, 1979), 8–15.

Smallwood, P., *Modern Critics in Practice: Critical Portraits of British Literary Critics* (London, 1990).

Sutherland, J.A., *Fiction and the Fiction Industry* (London, 1978). Discusses Lodge as a novelist of academic life.

Taylor, D.J., *After the War: The Novel and English Society Since 1945* (London, 1993). Includes scattered idiosyncratic comments on Lodge; praises *The Picturegoers*.

Widdowson, P., 'The Anti-History Men: Malcolm Bradbury and David Lodge', *Critical Quarterly* (Winter, 1984), 5–32.

Woodman, T., *Faithful Fictions: The Catholic Novel in British Literature* (Milton Keynes, 1991). A useful study, which considers Lodge's Catholic aspects in their larger literary context.

Index

Amis, Kingsley, 14, 31
  Lucky Jim, 14
Angry Young Men, 4
Ariosto, Lodovico, 20–21, 46
  Orlando Furioso, 20–21
Arnold, Matthew, 50
Austen, Jane, 16, 17, 18, 49, 56
  Northanger Abbey, 17–18

Bahktin, Mikhail, 17, 50, 52, 55–56, 59
Barthes, Roland, 51
Beckett, Samuel, 61
Belloc, Hilaire, 50
Bellow, Saul, 58–59
  Herzog, 58-59
Blake, William 16
Bloom, Harold, 7
Booth, Wayne, C., 37
  The Rhetoric of Fiction, 37
Bradbury, Malcom, 5
Braine, John, 29
Brontë, Charlotte, 49
Burgess, Anthony, 29
Burroughs, William, 50

Carlyle, Thomas, 25
Chaucer, Geoffrey, 19
  Canterbury Tales, 19
Cervantes, Miguel de, 35

Chesterton, G. K., 20, 29, 50
Conrad, Joseph, 7
Corvo, Baron (F. W. Rolfe), 7–8, 32
Culler, Jonathan, 15
  Structuralist Poetics, 15

Derrida, Jacques, 52
Dickens, Charles, 25, 31, 47, 49, 57–58
  Hard Times, 25, 28
  Martin Chuzzlewit, 47, 58
Disraeli, Benjamin, 25
  Sybil, 25
Dostoevsky, Fyodor, 55

Eco, Umberto, 22, 55
Eliot, George, 57
Eliot, T. S., 16, 21, 48
  The Waste Land, 21, 54
Empson, William, 48

Fielding, Henry, 35, 37, 60
  Tom Jones, 37
Forster, E. M., 48
Foucault, Michel, 52
Frye, Northrop, 22

Gaskell, Elizabeth, 25
  North and South, 25

Genette, Gerard, 55
Gissing, George, 11, 27
Greene, Graham, 2–4, 7–8, 29–31, 35, 43, 50, 57, 58
    Brighton Rock, 3
    The Quiet American, 4

Haffenden, John, 20
Hardy, Thomas, 49, 54, 57
Hawthorne, Nathaniel, 19
Heller, Joseph, 59
Hemingway, Ernest, 7, 50, 54
Hopkins, G. M., 29
Hughes, Ted, 55
    Crow, 55

Jakobsen, Roman, 52
James, Henry, 7–8, 11, 34, 48, 49–50, 56–57, 60
    The Ambassadors, 49–50
John XXIII, Pope, 33
John Paul II, Pope, 39
Johnson, Samuel, 45
Jones, David, 29
Joyce, James, 2, 7–9, 11, 29, 31, 54, 59, 60
    Dubliners, 9
    Finnegans Wake, 54
    A Portrait of the Artist as a Young Man, 9, 11, 30
    'The Sisters', 54
    Ulysees, 2, 6–8, 54

Kafka, Franz, 7
Kierkegaard, Søren, 59
Knight, G. Wilson, 49

Lawrence, D. H., 7, 11
    Sons and Lovers, 11
Leavis, F. R., 25, 50, 51
Lévi-Strauss, Claude, 52
Lehmann, Rosamond, 13
    Dusty Answer, 13
Lerner, Laurence, 50

The Truthtellers, 50
Lodge, David,
    'Adapting *Nice Work* for Television', 58
    After Bakhtin, 55-56
    'Ambiguously Ever After', 54
    The Art of Fiction, 56–57, 60
    'The Bowling Alley and the Sun', 12
    The British Museum is Falling Down, 1, 5–8, 31–34, 38
    Changing Places, 12, 14–18, 20, 23, 44
    Ginger, You're Barmy, 1, 3–5, 31, 58
    How Far Can You Go?, 33-41, 43-46, 51
    Language of Fiction, 14, 48–50, 54
    'Memories of a Catholic Childhood', 29–30
    'Mimesis and Diegesis in Modern Fiction', 56
    The Modes of Modern Writing, 51–56
    The Novelist at the Crossroads, 50-51
    Nice Work, 14–15, 23, 41, 43, 45, 52, 53
    Out of the Shelter, 1, 8–12, 23, 40
    Paradise News, 39–44, 46, 59
    'Pay As You Learn', 28
    The Picturegoers, 1–3, 5, 9, 31, 33, 39–40, 43
    Small World, 14, 18–23, 39, 44, 45, 51
    Therapy, 45–46, 58–59
    Working with Structuralism, 51-55

The Writing Game, 58
Lubbock, Percy, 48

Mackenzie, Compton, 13
    Sinister Street, 13
Mailer, Norman, 59
Mauriac, François, 30
Moseley, Merritt, 11, 34

New Criticism, 48–49, 51–52
Newman, J. H., 29
Nietzsche, F. W., 16

Orwell, George, 11

Paul VI, Pope, 33
    Humanae Vitae, 33–34,
    36, 38
Plato, 56
poststructuralism, 19, 38, 52,
    55

Rabelais, François, 55
Richards, I. A., 48
Rock Around the Clock, 3

Salinger, J. D., 59
Saussure, Ferdinand de, 54
Scholes, Robert, 54
Shakespeare, William, 22, 42,
    45–46, 49, 61
    The Tempest, 42
Sillitoe, Alan, 1

*Saturday Night and
    Sunday Morning*, 1
Snow, C. P., 7
Song of Bernadette, 2
Spark, Muriel, 29, 50
Spenser, Edmund, 21
    The Faerie Queen, 21
structuralism, 15, 49, 50–56
Swift, Jonathan, 16

Tallis, Raymond, 54
Thackeray, W. M., 13, 35
    Pendennis, 13
    Vanity Fair, 35
Thatcher, Margaret, 23, 36
Todorov, Tzvetan, 52, 55
Tristram Shandy, 50
Twain, Mark, 16, 59

Updike, John, 50

Vatican II, 32-33, 37

Waugh, Evelyn, 13, 29, 33,
    54, 57
    Brideshead Revisited, 13
    Decline and Fall, 13
Wells, H. G., 11, 49, 60
Widdowson, Peter, 44, 46
Wolfe, Tom, 55
Woolf, Virgina, 7, 48

Zola, Emile, 27